DIVIDED WORLD

notionpress.com

INDIA · SINGAPORE · MALAYSIA

Notion Press

No.8, 3rd Cross Street
CIT Colony, Mylapore
Chennai, Tamil Nadu – 600004

First Published by Notion Press 2020
Copyright © Binod Kumar Gogoi 2020
All Rights Reserved.

ISBN 978-1-64983-804-9

IN SEARCH OF AN
ELUSIVE CONSENSUS

DIVIDED WORLD

FINDING UNITY
AMONG GLOBAL DISARRAY

BINOD KUMAR GOGOI

INDIA • SINGAPORE • MALAYSIA

INDICACADEMY

INDIC PLEDGE

- *I celebrate our civilisational identity, continuity & legacy in thought, word and deed.*

- *I believe our indigenous thought has solutions for the global challenges of health, happiness, peace and sustainability.*

- *I shall seek to preserve, protect and promote this heritage and in doing so,*
  - *discover, nurture and harness my potential,*
  - *connect, cooperate and collaborate with fellow seekers,*
  - *advance diversity and inclusivity in the society.*

ABOUT INDIC ACADEMY

Indic Academy is a non-traditional 'university' for traditional knowledge. We seek to bring about a global renaissance based on Indic civilizational and indigenous thought. We are pursuing a multidimensional strategy across time, space and cause by establishing centers of excellence, transforming intellectuals and building an ecosystem.

Indic Academy is pleased to support this book.

FORE PAGE

"Man has lost the capacity to foresee and to forestall. He will end by destroying the earth."

– Albert Schweitzer

"The sedge is withered from the lake, and no birds sing."

– John Keats

This book is dedicated to my son, Arunav, and daughter, Aditi, and my grandchildren, Tanmay and Ipsita, without whom my life would have been barren and forlorn.

AUTHOR

CONTENTS

PREFACE

This book is the consummation of my long-cherished desire to write a book on the burning issues of the world that confront us today. Meanwhile, I have written several articles and poems both in Assamese and English dailies in Assam and in our neighbouring state Meghalaya. I have chosen *Divided World* as the title of the book for specific reasons. I was a child when India attained freedom and, as a result, the tragic heart-rending event of Partition took place. The memory of Partition still troubles us sometimes, because as I grew up, I came to know the evils of Partition and the consequences that followed. Now, however, I realise that it was not only India that was divided but it is also the whole world that is divided because of situations that are unfolding before us day by day.

Our age is called the Atomic Age as well as the Cyber Age with new and newer fields of science and technology and everchanging innovations in the day-to-day lives of the people. However, as days pass and years roll by, human beings are beset with newer and newer problems created by ourselves due to the misuse of science and technology. A day will come, as I perceive, when human beings will be overwhelmed and controlled by the machines we make. This is the emerging situation in the world with regard to the burning issues confronting us, like nuclear disarmament, terrorism, climate change and even topics like trade and commerce.

The nations of the world, even under the good offices of an august body like the UNO, are unable to come to terms. This shows the prevailing divisive politics and diplomacy in this troubled world.

This book is an attempt to search for a consensus on the vexing problems that until now defy any tangible solution.

As regards global warming and resultant climate change, Nobel Laureate Al Gore believes that one of the best ways to bring down emission levels is to levy a carbon tax based on consumption. Many European countries have adopted such a tax. Some of them have estimated that the social cost of carbon, as it is called, was equivalent to 843 dollars per tonne of carbon.

In India, though per capita emissions are still low, especially in rural areas, it may be worth exploring imposing such a tax on industries linked to the consumption or use of carbon-emitting goods. India already levies a heavy tax on petrol but that is more as a revenue measure rather than to discourage consumption.

Trading with carbon consumption will emerge as a huge business if a new global pact is reached. India already accounts for 32% of the projects established under what is known as the Clean Development Mechanism (CDM). Known as the cap and trade system, it allows companies in developed countries to meet their emission targets by buying credits from units that pollute less or by investing in CDM projects in developing countries.

Looking at the day-to-day events around the world, it appears to my mind that the old Cold War mentality is still simmering in the nations of the world. The main players in these power games seem to be of three groups – the first led by the USA and its allies like Saudi Arabia, the second led by ex-superpower Russia and its friendly allies and the third led by the emerging superpower China, with enormous military and economic power along with tremendous diplomatic clout.

There seems to be a void in the international power scenario in view of the exit of one of the stalwarts of the European Union, England. Therefore, there is an interplay of forces to fill up the void. Once, there was talk of Greater European solidarity as visualised by Ex-President of Russia, Mikhail Gorbachev, of a Pan-European Confederation from Lisbon to East Russian Vladivostok. However, that ideal fell through and eventually did not materialise.

But now, NATO seems to be tottering and dithering because of simmering discontent and dissatisfaction among the members of the organisation. In the event of any destabilisation in Ukraine owing to civil disorders, Russia may step in and emerge with new strength and vitality. In such a situation, Russia will be destined to play a decisive role in the vast Euro-Asian region. This will give a further boost to China in its quest for superpower status. In this global context, India will have to be the moderator or balancer in international power politics in this everchanging troubled world.

Under such circumstances, India should put forward its demands more forcefully and vehemently in the UNO General Assembly and the Security Council. Nobody can block or silence the voice of one hundred and thirty crore people forever.

As regards disarmament or non-proliferation of nuclear weapons, if the UNO fails to take the leadership, let the Non-Aligned Movement (NAM) be revamped, which is now in a dormant position, to take urgent and effective measures so that differences among nations may be ironed out and action may be taken in this regard. According to the Russian foreign minister, due steps should be taken timely to conclude a SALT II (Strategic Arms Limitation Talks) treaty to check the further spread of atomic weapons, like the Intercontinental Ballistic Missiles (ICBM), and the like to solve the vexing problem of durable peace and harmony among the comity of nations.

In the midst of a murky atmosphere prevailing throughout the world, who will be the conscious keeper in the world affairs where divisive politics and intricate diplomacy are at work? To my mind, the

UNO, particularly the member nations, must exert timely pressure and save the world from extinction. Voices of the members of the UNO will have to be vigorously reinforced by informed and enlightened public opinions of the saner sections of the people around the world.

At the moment, two primary hot spots in West Asia have become perennial sources of tension and renewed confrontation. One is the North-West Syrian city Idlib and the other is the Israeli-Palestinian conflict. Both are conflicts involving highly humanitarian considerations. At present, no imminent solution to these conflicts is in sight. While Turkey and Russia on their part are engaged in weeding out militants from the region, because of the incessant bombing by the government forces led by Assad (President of Syria), backed by Russia, there has lately been an exodus of people to nearby Turkey, which is already overburdened by 3.5 million refugees. This unprecedented situation has compelled Turkish authorities to open the floodgates of refugees to Europe. No doubt, given such a humanitarian crisis, NATO (North Atlantic Treaty Organization) has urged the parties concerned to halt further bombing in the region and declare an immediate ceasefire so that the region is not engulfed in a full-fledged war.

As regards the conflict between Israel and Palestine, a policy of perpetual peace and harmony is needed, which calls for statesmanship and sagacity in both sides of leadership. I think dismantling the artificial wall in the occupied territories will pave the way for a change of hearts among the people. No doubt, the existence of the wall leads to severe disruption of Palestinian lives. According to a UNO report, there has been a decrease of more than 80% in the number of farmers who cultivate their lands and a decline of 60% of the yields of olive orchards.

These are the harmful effects of the wall. We can only hope that both sides will try their best to hammer out a workable and reasonable solution of their contentious problem in a spirit of give and take in accordance with the Security Council Resolution 242 of November 22,

1967, Resolution 338 of October 22, 1973, and Resolution 446 of March 22, 1979. I believe that the two-nation concept will be the best and most viable solution of the never-ending conflict for sustained and durable peace and harmony in the region.

As regards our own country, which is said to be a union of states as declared under Article 3 of the Constitution of India, let it be declared afresh by way of an amendment of the Constitution as an indestructible union of indestructible states in line with the idealism ingrained in the basic feature of the US Constitution. Prior to this declaration, all our existing union territories should be so organised as to be economically and administratively viable to be recognised as states. We should put a stop to further Balkanisation of states. Otherwise, separatist tendencies will have the upper hand, which the fathers of our constitution did not anticipate at the time of drafting the Constitution.

CHAPTER 1

DECLINE OF DEMOCRACY & THE PARLIAMENT

Before World War I, the people in the West revered the most prominent intellectuals of the times like Goethe, Immanuel Kant, Bertrand Russell, Arnold Toynbee and the like but they had to face hard and agonising days.[1]

Their legacy has been passed on from generations to generations. However, not everybody of their ilk toed the line of the government of the day. As a result, some of them were imprisoned, notable among whom were towering personalities like Russell, Eugene Debs, etc. They were sentenced to undergo years of imprisonment.

---

1   Goethe. J. W. (1849–1932) was a renowned man of letters in the 19th century. His famous finest works are Faust and Wilhelm Meister's Apprenticeship.

Arnold Toynbee (1889–1975) was an eminent historian and strong advocate of World Government. His 12-volume *A Study of History* is an international classic. These books attempt to trace the rise and fall of civilizations.

Bertrand Russell (1872–1970) was a British philosopher and mathematician, famous for his radical views. He wrote more than fifty books, which include *History of Western Philosophy, Human Society in Ethics and Politics, Portraits from Memory* and *Wisdom of the West*. He was a moving spirit and the founder and president of various bodies working for world peace. He campaigning against the making and testing of nuclear weapons. He was awarded the Order of Merit in 1949 and the Nobel Prize for literature in 1950. He also received the Kalinga Prize for popularization of science.

The reason was the questions they raised about President Wilson's[2] war with concern to democracy and human rights.

These scholars were particularly concerned about what they called the excesses of democracy like atrocities committed on minorities, working people, women, young and old. They called for moderation and fair play in a democratic system of government. However, in spite of the excess of democracy, President Truman[3] had been able to govern well with the cooperation of a relatively small number of Wall Street lawyers and bankers and democracy flourished.

There are certain drawbacks in the democratic setup. Here some of the marginalised sections of the population remained unrepresented in the state legislatures and National Parliament because there are various major castes and numerous sub-castes who are not adequately represented in these public institutions. Hence, they have to remain content without having a say in policy-making and decision-making, which directly or indirectly affects their lives. So at the time of local or general elections, a mechanism should be devised so that these neglected sections of the communities can send their own representatives to the state legislatures and the Parliament. This will surely mitigate the grievances of these deprived and marginalised sections.

---

2   Woodrow Wilson (1856–1924) was the 28th President of the USA during 1913–21. He was primarily instrumental and responsible for the victories of the Allies during World War I. He was awarded the coveted Nobel Peace Prize in 1919. His famous Fourteen Points became the very basis for future peace in the world.

3   Harry S. Truman (1888–1972) was President of the USA for the term 1945–1952. He put an end to the World War II by dropping atom bombs over Japan. After the war, he initiated the rehabilitation of Europe and launched technical assistance programmes for developing countries. His shrewdness and common sense were responsible for the success of the well-known Marshall Plan.

Sometimes it is seen that well-established interest groups and pressure groups become helpless when their grievances are not adequately addressed or listened to. Actually, power must not reside in the hands of the economic elites alone. The time-honoured maxim, 'Will, not force, is the basis of state' should be kept in view.

Political leaders sometimes tend to subserve their own electoral interest unmindful of the broad interests of the people they represent. India's greatest tragedy is eloquently depicted by the late Nani Palkhivala[4] in his well-read book *We, the Nation.*

In this memorable book, he said: "The greatest problem of India is that its finest men – men of calibre and vision, knowledge and character are not in politics and stand little chance of getting elected having regard to the murky atmosphere of our political life."

Really, our leaders should not have fossilised mindsets and they should have a broad vision and forward-looking attitude tempered by a clear ideology and outlook.

One of the makers of New India, our first Prime Minister, Jawaharlal Nehru[5], once said, "A caste-ridden society is not properly secular. When

---

4   Author of widely read book *We, the Nation*, Nani Palkhivala was a much-admired lawyer in the field of jurisprudence and much sought after constitution lawyer. He was very concerned about our present-day society and was critical about the ills of present-day society, the political system and government. He was a strong advocate of human rights and was imbued with a deep sense of social welfare and justice.

5   Jawaharlal Nehru (1889 –1964) was the Prime Minister of India from 1947 to May 27, 1964. He was a noted author and fluent speaker, great politician and visionary and honest statesman. He was President of the Indian National Congress during the period 1929 –30, 1952–53. He was an ardent believer in secularism, the Policy of Non-Alignment and peaceful co- existence. He attained worldwide fame for his high ideals, principles and political sagacity.

a person's beliefs become petrified in caste divisions they affect the social structure of the state and prevent us from realising the idea of equality which we claim to place before all else."

Jeremy Bentham[6] is also known to have said that the government shall always be insulated by what is described as, "The greatest happiness of the greatest number."

Democracy always happens to be a government that is run by parties on party lines. But then parties organised primarily on caste basis are bound to be sectarian and not universal in catering to the hopes and aspirations of every section of the population.

The absence of mass-based egalitarian party organisation may do harm to a parliamentary system of government and violently erode the credibility of the people. Even in the developed countries of Europe today we see a perceptible decline of democracy as a system of government and a way of life. Notably, in countries like Greece, a celebration of democracy of the bygone days, things are not all right and the whole social fabric there seems to be torn to pieces because of the economic downturns.

---

6   He was the real founder of the Utilitarian school of political philosophy. He revolutionized industry in England. Born in 1748, Bentham was an intellectual prodigy who went to Oxford but later entertained a poor opinion of education he received there. From Oxford, he went to Lincoln's Inn in London to receive his legal training. Bentham had a scientific bent of mind, given to introspection. From a comparatively early age, he was given to tackling problems of social welfare. From Priestley's *Essay on Government*, Bentham learnt that the true end of the state was to promote happiness of the greatest number. A state and its laws were good or bad according to the extent they kept this end in view. In 1776, Bentham wrote his A *Fragment on Government*, advocating change in the government and laws in England, which brought him into contact with the ardent reformers and politicians of his day. His interest in the theory of jurisprudence and his zeal for legal reform kept up until his death in 1832.

It is seen that highly monopolised economies cannot deliver justice and equality in a country unless it is infused with altruism.

It is unfortunate that from time to time during elections, whether local or national, sometimes divisive politics are at work to pollute the political atmosphere and reap electoral benefits. Such tendencies should be abjured in the interest of fair democratic elections.

If democracy happens to be in peril, society or community itself will be in peril. If one happens to look into the day-to-day proceedings of Parliament, one is dismayed to see the performance of some of the members of the House. Sometimes the speeches seem to be perfunctory, lacking a sense of involvement. No doubt, there are reputed and very responsible members in both Houses of Parliament who are men of wisdom and common sense. One is really delighted to listen to such debates or speeches, though such scenes are rare. Sometimes, debates are avoided for lack of time. Sometimes bills meant for the public good are rarely thoroughly discussed in the Houses and are passed in haste, which is undesirable. Matters of great public importance should be given due importance and there should be a detailed exhaustive discussion.

The control of public expenditure in the Indian democracy is exercised by the Parliament through parliamentary committees, the Finance Ministry and the Comptroller and Auditor General. Of all the committees in the Parliament, the Estimates Committee and the Public Accounts Committee stand apart, exercising unique financial control and powers not shared by other standing committees in Parliament.

The main business of the Estimates Committee is to suggest as to how the policy and objectives of the government could be carried out with the least expenditure of public resources.

It suggests policies to bring about efficiency and economy in administration so that the money is well laid out within the limits of the policy implied in the estimates.

In fact, the committee examines the current government activity in light of how it costs the public.

As regards the Public Accounts Committee, it examines the Report of the Comptroller and Auditor General in order to find out whether the money voted by Parliament has been properly utilised by the authority. It examines whether public expenditure exceeds the appropriation granted by Parliament without its prior approval. It also examines whether a grant is utilised for the purpose for which it was sanctioned.

According to T. N. Chaturvedi, a former CAG (Comptroller And Auditor General), "The follow-up action on the PAC Report is lackadaisical and evasive. The government has the support of the party and they consider any criticism to be a fault of the party instead of the administration. Therefore, PAC (Public Accounts Committee) and other parliamentary committees are losing their edge."

Besides, in the Parliament, there are various committees and select committees. For example, there is a committee on the ministers' assurances. This particular committee is rarely utilised and no one even raises questions in the House as to the fulfilment of assurances given by ministers.

It happens that sometimes attendance in the Parliament is very thin and irregular for which the House itself has to be adjourned by the speaker for lack of quorum. This is indeed unfortunate and speaks of the poor functioning of parliamentary democracy.

Defection is another evil that spoils the political system and badly eats into the vitality of the democratic edifice on which the whole system of government rests. In spite of my fading memory, I still remember to have read a piece on Gandhian thought in the distant past where he advocated for blending religion with politics to realise idealism and spiritualism even in the sphere of politics.

No doubt, in a parliamentary system of government, the speaker enjoys a pre-eminent position. In view of his exalted position and status, he should always be neutral and non-partisan in the conduct of the proceedings of the House. He is the custodian of not only the rules and regulations of the House but also the rights and privileges of the members of the House. Moreover, he is the main custodian of the dignity and decorum of the House that he presides over, enjoying an undisputed and exalted position.

Everyone in the House looks to him for advice and guidance for the true and faithful interpretation of the rules of the House whenever any point of order is raised by any honourable member of the House.

So the success of parliamentary democracy depends very much on the ability and knowledge of the speaker as well as how he manages the day-to-day affairs of the House.

According to Ivor Jennings[7], a parliamentary system means a cabinet system of government, which is a government of limited powers, and it has to act in accordance with the rule of law, which must not be transgressed under any circumstances.

Under such a government, the Council of Ministers, whether they belong to the states or the centre is individually and collectively responsible to the House, be it the Legislative Assembly or the Parliament. Therefore, the Council of Ministers, headed by the prime minister at the

---

7   He was a widely known political scientist. He authored the widely known, read and deeply admired *The Cabinet Government*, in which he analyses as to how the work of the government is carried on and how it will have to work according to the rule of the law. Here in the book he also deals with the limits within which a cabinet system of government functions.

centre or the chief minister, owes its allegiance to the House and, as such, it is to function as a coherent team. However, sometimes it is seen that the Council fails to adhere to this principle because of a conflict of interest, which must be avoided. Such a state of affairs may erode the confidence of the people in the system itself and seriously damage the credibility of the cabinet system of government.

In this connection, the words of John Stuart Mill[8] are worth mentioning as relevant: "The only purpose for which power can be rightly exercised over any member of civilised society against his will is to prevent them from harm to others."

Very recently, the Supreme Court of India's directive to a floor test of the Devendra Fadnavis Government upon a petition by the three parties consisting of Siva Sena, NCP (Nationalist Congress Party) and INC (Indian National Congress) parties challenging the formation of the BJP Government is a victory of democracy and the vindication of just and fair constitutional principles and practices. This decision of the Apex Court paved the way for the party alliance of the three parties and on 28 November 2019, Uddhav Thackeray was sworn in as the 18th Chief Minister of Maharashtra. It proves once again that ideologically different alliances are nothing new in Indian politics.

---

8   J. S Mill (1806–1873) was trained by his father James Mill and by John Austin. In his early days, he was influenced by Bentham's utilitarian philosophy and its reforming programmes. J. S Mill was of the opinion that happiness of man cannot be sought as an end in itself. Cultivation of feeling is necessary for proper development of man.

CHAPTER 2

INDIA ITSELF WAS DIVIDED

We are now living in a world broken, fragmented and thus divided. This world is already divided geographically, which is natural. We have the continents and the oceans and seas that separate us naturally. But unfortunately, now the separation seems to be based on regionalism, ethnicity, religion, national security or what one may call national self-interest. Long ago, the notable reputed writer Hans Morgenthau acknowledged that a nation's policies in the international affairs are largely determined by national self-interest. This is true. However, this is also true that there are no permanent friends and permanent enemies in international relations. Yesterday's enemies may be today's friends. This view is shared by no lesser a personality than Thant, the former Secretary-General of the UNO. However, now, all nations of the world are divided on major issues under the sun.

In the past, our intellectual philosophers and leaders like M. K Gandhi, Dr S. Radhakrishnan, Arnold Toynbee, Bertrand Russell, Albert Einstein, Rabindranath Tagore, Max Mueller and a host of others talked of one living under a World Government, World Parliament and World Judiciary. Gandhi himself talked of such a possibility. He usually recited this concept as visualised by his slogan '*Jai Jagat*' (Victory to the World), which is not lesser than a victory of humanity.

This is, however, true that in a world divided by so many barriers, the concept of world government will never materialise. The national governments of the world may, however, iron out their differences in a peaceful manner without resort to blackmailing, threat or war. But now this is lacking in this world. Today the world is more divided politically, economically and even socially that one cannot even consider cohesive thinking.

As for India, it was itself divided into two parts because of Partition after independence in 1947. It was a tragic event shaped by history as well as destiny. The memory of Partition still lingers on because it thrives generations after generations. The sum total of these accumulated memories and events and sacrifices constitute what we call the soul of India.

Really, I am myself a child of Partition as I was just eight years old when Partition took place, though at that long distance of time as a child, I did not know the nitty-gritty of Partition. It would seem that independent India itself, 73 years old now, has not been able to shake off the memory or erase the scare of that momentous event, which was epoch-making, intriguing, political yet personal. The ghosts of Partition still are there in the shape of Jammu and Kashmir, which is in a melting pot, though it was long declared in the UNO as a closed chapter in its debates by the Ex-Defence Minister of India the late VK Krishna Menon.

No doubt, Mohammad Ali Jinnah was the ambassador of Hindu-Muslim unity, but subsequently, he took side with the Muslim League and became a separatist leader. Thus, he became the Father of Pakistan. Therefore, Partition became inevitable and it happened. It was definitely not a result of a clash of civilisation; rather it was primarily a clash of personalities and political circumstances occurring at that point of time for which Partition took place. The scene and the accompanying lurking ghosts of Partition are vividly reflected in the memorable words of Rama Chandra Guha, an intellectual and noted writer, in his noted book *India after Gandhi*: "Ten million refugees were on the move, on foot, by bullock carts and by train; sometimes travelling under army escorts, at other times, trusting to fate and their respective Gods.... This was without question the greatest mass migration in history."

It is worthwhile here to recapitulate some of the lingering doubts and misunderstandings arising out of the conflict of Jammu and Kashmir. When the paramountcy of the British Crown lapsed over India at midnight of August 14th, 1947, Lord Mountbatten, the last Viceroy of British India, declared: "My scheme leaves you with all the practical independence that you can possibly use and makes you free of all those subjects which you cannot possibly manage on your own."

This declaration gave Pakistan encouragement for their tribal population to indulge in raids and depredations that began on 22nd October 1947. The invasion of tribal people, aided and abetted by Pakistan, placed the government of Jammu and Kashmir in a very difficult predicament. On 27th October 1947, India accepted the Instrument of Accession from the Maharaja of Jammu and Kashmir and, as a result, it became an integral and inalienable part of India ever since. But for political rather than for constitutional reasons, India assured the people of Kashmir that accession would be subject to a plebiscite of the people. It was to be noted that the above declaration was made by then Prime Minister of India after the acceptance of the accession and accession was not made subject to that condition.

On 30th December 1947, India, under Article 35 of the Charter of the UNO, referred the dispute to the Security Council. In April 1948, the Security Council appointed a commission to be known as the UNO Commission for India and Pakistan for the restoration of peace and order. This commission adopted a resolution on August 13, 1948, containing a ceasefire and truce agreement. The ceasefire was accepted by both the governments and it became effective from midnight of January 1, 1949. The commission passed another resolution on January 5, 1949, signifying the acceptance by both the governments of the various principles incidental to the commission's resolution of 13th August

1948. It provided for the determination of the accession of Jammu and Kashmir to India or Pakistan to be declared through a plebiscite.

In pursuance of the second resolution, Admiral Chester Nimitz of the USA Navy was appointed by the Secretary-General of the UNO as the Plebiscite Administrator with the approval of the governments, with a view to expediting the holding of the plebiscite. The commission referred the problem to the UNO in December 1947 and recommended the appointment of an arbitrator. The Security Council appointed Sir Owen Dixon, a jurist and a judge of the High Court of Australia, as a mediator.

He could not iron out the differences between the two governments regarding the procedure for and extent of demilitarisation and the degree of control over administration necessary to ensure a plebiscite.

In April 1951, the Security Council appointed Dr Frank Graham, the then President of the University of North Carolina, as UNO Representative in Jammu and Kashmir to obtain the agreement of both India and Pakistan for demilitarisation. In accordance with his report, a conference at the ministerial level was convened in Geneva by Dr Graham on August 25, 1952, but the two governments differed on the conception of their status in Jammu and Kashmir.

In February 1954, the Jammu and Kashmir Constituent Assembly finally decided to accede to the Indian Union. Subsequently, through the President's order regarding Jammu and Kashmir, the jurisdiction of the Central Government was extended to all the subjects in the Union List.

It is noteworthy that the Instrument of Accession by which Jammu and Kashmir acceded to India was voluntary, although made at a critical time when the freedom of the state was in danger. This accession was further strengthened when Jammu and Kashmir sent its representatives to the Constituent Assembly and accepted the Constitution of India. It, therefore, became an integral part and a state of the Union of India. It was another matter that the then PM of India pledged to the people of Jammu and Kashmir that the accession could be reaffirmed by the people if they so desired. This undertaking has only a moral value; it has no semblance of any legal character. However, the first part of the joint undertaking between the two countries about the withdrawal of Pakistani troops was never given effect to. In this context, Ex-PM Jawaharlal Nehru commented, "We cannot wait forever before we take any action. There must be some finality to things."

On March 29, 1956, Nehru withdrew the offer of plebiscite on these grounds. Firstly, for a plebiscite to take place under the UNO Resolution, Pakistan failed to withdraw troops from Jammu and Kashmir. Secondly, the Jammu and Kashmir Constituent Assembly had approved the merger with India and accepted India's Constitution. Thirdly, because of Pakistan's alliances, the objective situation in the subcontinent had changed beyond redemption. By 1957, the then government dispensed with all its previous commitments and the accession of Jammu and Kashmir to India was decided once and for all.

Later on, it is noteworthy that Lee Hamilton, the then Chairman, Foreign Affairs Committee of the USA Congress, contended that the plebiscite mechanism in Jammu and Kashmir had been suspended by the Simla Agreement (1972) and that a political process between Delhi and the people of Jammu and Kashmir was essential to end the stalemate. He wanted division of Jammu and Kashmir along the line of control, which is significant and needs to be read between the lines.

Another Senator Bill Bradley commented at that time that a society as diverse as India would fragment if the plebiscite idea won. To him, it was a challenge posed not only to India and the USA but also to other countries of the world.

Division cannot be a unifying force, which is more welcome in a country in which heterogeneous communities co-exist with each other by maintaining unity in diversity. Do we want a fragmented or divided world? Do we want permanent enmity with our immediate neighbours, Pakistan and China? Now, let us see what Strobe Talbott, Ex. Deputy Secretary of State of America and President of the Brookings Institution, Washington, have to say about Pakistan vis-à-vis India: "I vividly recall Indian concerns about Talibanization and Afghanization of Pakistan during my own involvement in a dialogue with Jaswant Singh, the then foreign minister of India in the late 1990s. That danger was real then and it is more real today in some parts of that country. All parties with influence on the Pakistani government and influential forces in the country should use whatever persuasive powers they have to make the case that the biggest threat facing the long-term stability and even viability of the Pakistani State is not India – rather it is the rise of violent elements within Pakistan and along its borders with Afghanistan."

India's Partition cannot be understood apart from its global context, which was one of the most chaotic and uncertain of modern history. In the late 1930s and 40s, war raged across Europe and Asia. Empires were collapsing and states were brought under subjugation. There was a rise and fall of nations throughout the world. The whole world was, as if, in turmoil and in a melting pot.

"Empires, by definition, ruled over culturally and socially mixed people: their territories were aligned not to religious or linguistic identities, but through allegiance to an overarching symbol or idea. As empires retreated or were defeated, the spreading model of the nation-state tried to bring cultural and social identity into alignment with the territory. The transition occasioned much blood-shedding and generated the terminology of genocide, ethnic cleansing and of Partition."[9]

---

9   Op. Cit: Sunil Khilnani. India Today. August 31, 2009.

It was a time when minorities across the world were struggling for their national identities, a place under the sun as seen among Arabs and the Jews in Palestine. In such an environment, the Indian predicament was unique and was part of a global one. As far back as 1942, a prominent Congress leader, the late Chakravarti Rajagopalachari, better known as Rajaji, recognised the legitimacy of Pakistan for safeguarding rights of the Indian Muslims under the principle of regional self-determination. This idea was, however, vehemently opposed by Pandit Nehru, who insisted on a strong centre, whereas Mr Jinnah was for maximum autonomy. In short, it may be concluded that the Partition occurred in the Indian subcontinent because of circumstances consequent to the end of the Second World War in 1945, with the ever-rising tide of nationalistic feelings. It may also be due to the persistent clash of egos, ideas and personalities. As for Jinnah, he always insisted on parity and equality.

Pakistan was founded on the assumption that nationhood would ensure such parity in the subcontinent. But Pakistan's subsequent history has been a bitter lesson in the fact that not all states are equal. It made Pakistan perpetually dependent on some external third party – the UNO, USA, China – as if as a go-between to assert for parity in between the two nations. It is because of this mindset that Pakistani leaders are obsessed with nuclear weapons.

In a recent interview with Al Jazeera, Imran Khan, the Prime Minister of Pakistan, declared that there is ample prospect of war in the wake of India's, what he called, "Illegal annexation of Kashmir." The prime minister tacitly acknowledged that Pakistan could lose in a conventional war with India, and in that case, there could be consequences."

Regarding issuing a nuclear threat to India over Kashmir, he told the channel, "There is no confusion; what I said is that Pakistan will never start a nuclear war. I am a pacifist. I am anti-war. I believe that war does not solve problems."

War has unintended consequences. Look at Vietnam or Iraq: the wars caused other problems much more than what they were originally waged for. But I am clear that when two nuclear-armed countries fight a conventional war, there is every possibility of it ending in a nuclear war. If I say Pakistan, God forbid, is in a conventional war and it is losing, then like any country stuck between choices of either surrendering or fighting to the death for its freedom, I know that Pakistan will fight to the death for freedom. That is why we approached the UNO and we are approaching every international forum so that they act right now as this is a potential disaster that will go way beyond the Indian subcontinent.

Ex-Indian Foreign Minister Subrahmanyam Jaishankar was on a three-day visit to Finland and met the Chairman of the European Union who supported India on Kashmir. During a special debate of the plenary session of European Parliamentarians, Ryszard Czarnecki and Fulvio Martusciello attacked Pakistan for harbouring terrorism.

Czarnecki, a member of European Parliament and Euro Conservative and Reformist Group in Poland, called India the greatest democracy of the world and said terrorists who attacked India did not come from the moon. Later, delivering a lecture on India and world priorities of India's foreign policy at the Finnish Institute of International Affairs, Jaishankar said that India's decision to revoke Jammu and Kashmir's status had a national security connotation stressing that the epicentre of global terrorism is right there in the country's neighbourhood. It had been trying to internationalise the Jammu and Kashmir issue but India asserted that abrogation of Article 370 was its internal matter.[10]

As for India's idealism and future dream, it is amply reflected in Justice K. N Saikia Memorial Day Lecture delivered recently by former

---

10 S. Jaishankar, Foreign Minister of India; Speech in Finland.

President of India Pranab Mukherjee: "The soul of India resides in pluralism and celebration of diversity. This plurality of our society has come through assimilation of ideas over centuries. Secularism and inclusiveness are a matter of faith for us. It is our composite culture that makes us a nation. Every time an individual, a child or a woman is brutalised, the soul of India is wounded. Manifestations of rage are tearing our social fabric.[11]"

As for diplomacy, since the Barrack Obama days, it was best summed up by Stephen Cohen of the Brooking Institution: "This America is more open, more flexible and more true to itself than at any other time. There is a rare convergence of interests between the USA and India, whether it is on energy, terrorism or environment."

To quote from the speech of Obama, former President of America, "It is a world without justice and where ancient hatreds we still combat, as in the Middle East. It is a world where the war against civilisation is waged in the name of God. Mumbai being its latest site. We will not apologise for our way of life, nor will we waver in its defence. And for those who seek to address their aims by inducing terror and slaughtering innocents, we say to you now that our spirit is stronger and cannot be broken. You cannot outlast us and we will defeat you."[12]

Thus, what we need in this subcontinent of ours, which is our homeland, is a congenial inner environment that can cater to our common peace and happiness without which we cannot live. This whole apparatus of our life we call civilisation. Civilisation is the outer manifestation of what we actually think and do in our policy and actions. Civilisation expresses itself in politics, in economics, in

---

11   Pranab Mukherjee's speech in Guwahati, Justice K. N Saikia Memorial. The Assam Tribune 21.10.19.

12   Obama, Ex- President of USA. Speech in Delhi as quoted by S. Prasanna Rajan. India Today. Feb 2, 2009.

technology, while our culture expresses itself in art, in literature, in religion, even in our thoughts and philosophy. To quote the penetrating words of the eminent thinker and philosopher Bertrand Russell: "Mankind has become so much one family that we cannot insure our own prosperity except by insuring that of everyone else. If you wish to be happy, you must resign yourself to seeing others happy too. Contempt to happiness is usually contempt for other people's happiness and is an elegant disguise for the hatred of the human race."[13]

The present troubled world needs Gandhiji's example. This remark was made by Scottish artist Philip Jackson at Parliament Square in London. "Gandhi showed that you could win your argument and impose your will by peaceful means and in this troubled world that is an example to be followed." He also said that he was doubly honoured at being the one to execute the project in 2015 at the Parliament Square, "...already home to world leaders such as Nelson Mandela and Winston Churchill."[14]

Though I am now already above eighty, yet I do remember the memorable words of wisdom uttered by no less a person than the then President of America, Barack Obama, at the end of his visit to India during January 2015. It is still fresh in my memory that he addressed a gathering at Siri Fort Auditorium in New Delhi. He encouraged the audience, mostly young new generation Indians, to rise up and do their best to develop India as one of the most powerful nations of the world.

He said that India would progress if it were not splintered on religious lines. He remarked that like the USA, India is a secular nation having diverse religion, races, languages. He said, "We are the flowers of the same garden." He recollected Gandhiji, paid glowing tributes to

---

13   Bertrand Russell: British Philosopher and Mathematician. He wrote books on ethics and politics.

14   Philip Jackson: The Scottish artist of iconic sculpture.

him and said that all the nations of the world should imbibe the spirit of non-violence.

Days of superpower rivalry are gone. Multilateralism has come to stay. Today, international relations among nations play a decisive role. Here diplomacy occupies the pivotal role. There has been alignment and realignment of the nations as political players. The guiding principle is mutual self-interests of nations, which may be economic, political and strategic related to security concerns. Today, no nation or group of nations wants to remain isolated from others in the international sphere, because nations are bound to be dependent on each other for the realisation of their mutual objectives.

Ours is not only an Atomic Age but also a Cyber Age in which there is a rapid transmission of news and views instantaneously through the world. Hence, states need to keep themselves informed of the events of the world which may occur in far-flung lands but which may impact a nation in one way or the other.

In a major policy address to the International Democratic Union, Republican Senator Mitt Romney said that a balanced analysis of China leads to three possible futures:

first, China becomes the sole global superpower by the middle of the present century.

Second, China's rise or accession may be disrupted or halted by internal turmoil.

Third, China may be dissuaded from making global domination and instead becomes a responsible member of the global order. These are only propositions or possibilities.

However, the first proposition is most likely because of what China is doing at the moment. China has a comprehensive, rigorous strategy to achieve global domination. We are aware of its practices of forced technology transfer from any company seeking its markets, which is an outright technology theft. He said cyber spying and counterfeiting are vehicles for technology theft. We recently abandoned the Trans-Pacific Partnership. China lacks energy and raw materials. They are addressing them through their Belt and Road Initiative. And China has a history of revolution. This they are addressing in ways reminiscent of repressive regimes in world history armed with modern technology.

We should confront China together not alone, on its trade practices, insisting that counterfeiting technology theft, predatory pricing, subsidisation and market denial must cease immediately or we will lose free access to our markets. Products with military application should be sourced only from free countries. Insisting on fair trade practices is not hostility, but is sanity.[15]

Since taking office as the American President, Donald Trump has drastically changed his policy initiative in the Middle East by acceding to a string of Israeli demands and all but slamming the door on Palestinians.

This includes his major policy decision of recognising the disputed city of Jerusalem as Israel's capital and also Golan Heights, a territory taken from Syria in 1967 war.

In November, in another major and far-reaching development, the Trump administration broke off decades of international consensus as well as the verdict of the International Court of Justice when it maintained that it would no longer consider Israeli settlements on the occupied Palestinian lands in the West Bank illegal. These changed policies of Trump are highly popular with the right-wing Evangelical Christian Republicans – a vital part of Trump's electoral base, but pregnant with dangerous possibilities in the future.

---

15   ASSAM. TRIBUNE. 7 December, 2019

As for volatile North-East India, nothing should be done to impair the prevailing peace and harmony of the region – anything that may jeopardise the integrity and brotherhood existing among the various communities, social and religious groups in this region. No one should play divisive politics in this vital and strategic region for political gains. Otherwise, the whole region may turn into another Hong Kong or Vietnam, which will invite foreign intervention. This calls for political wisdom, statesmanship and political sagacity without which a harmonious and inclusive economic development cannot take place. The people of the North-East must not be compelled to suffer from our history for all times to come.

CHAPTER 3

GLOBAL WARMING VIS-À-VIS CLIMATE CHANGE

As on trade and commerce, nuclear weapons or issues like terrorism, even on burning issues like global warming and consequent climate change, most of the nations of the world are divided and do not speak in the same voice. They seem to take divergent views on these burning topics. This is the root cause for delaying on a comprehensive action plan to mitigate the ill effect of ever-emerging climate change. It may be due to the clash of civilisations, due to the individual egos like that of the President of America, Donald Trump, or due to the clash of personal ties present at the various international conferences on climate change.

After the ignominious collapse of the Copenhagen Summit in 2009, Bolivia organised a World People's Conference on climate change with thirty-five thousand participants from 140 countries, not just representatives of governments but also members of civil society and activists of global warming and climate change. The conference produced a People's Agreement, which called for a sharp reduction of emissions and a Universal Declaration on the rights of Mother Earth. Establishing the rights of the planet was the key demand of indigenous communities all over the world. However, it was ridiculed and laughed at by some of the sophisticated Westerners; but unless we can acquire some of the indigenous sensibility, they are likely to have the last laugh – the laughter of grim despair ahead.[16]

---

16 Noam Chomsky: Who rules the world? P-99.

The central theme was that we seize the existential crisis of climate change to transform our failed ecosystem into something radically different.

Crises have been used by the right, by corporations and by elites to push through land grabs. It is impossible to deal with climate change without redistribution of wealth. We have to remove these social ills. The physical world is going to change radically. So either we can change our economic system or we can be changed forever for the worst.

The US President is trying to create a climate legacy, but at the same time, he has allowed Arctic drilling, leading to vast emissions. In India, there is less access to energy in rural areas. So coal-based plants cannot be avoided, solar investments notwithstanding.

The most blatant instance of thoughtlessness is the action of the US President when he pulled out of the Paris Climate Deal of 2015. Major polluters like China and India are not lagging behind in mining activities with the pretext of enhancing the quality of life of their citizens, which is contrary to the Paris Accord.

Jeremy Ely of the University of Sheffield in the UK stated: "Our research shows for the first time that surface melt water is getting beneath the glaciers in the Antarctic Peninsula causing short bursts of gliding towards the sea 100% faster than normal water." On climate change, Europe is doing something tangible; on the other hand, the richest and the most powerful country in the world, the USA, does not have the national policy for restricting the use of fossil fuel and does not have a policy of renewable energy targets. It is not that their population do not need it; it is the institutional structure that stands in the way and there is a wide gap between policy and opinion.

Greenland summer heat has broken all previous records this time as 440 billion tonnes of ice are said to have melted down in the ocean in recent times. The Amazon is on fire, so is Central Africa and Asia's

Indonesia and far-off Australia, where fires have occurred recently. Under such a situation, Swedish teenager climate activist Greta Thunberg led the world's biggest children's action plan in New York just before the UNO sponsored crucial Global Climate Action Summit. This worldwide action of the children was dubbed as the Global Climate Change Strike and aimed at mounting pressures on governments world over to take effective action for preventing further warming of the planet and to mitigate the impact of adverse climate change.

Teachers, educationists, scientists, environmentalists and sociologists the world over have extended support to this global programme of the children. All India People's Science Network at its General Council meeting held in New Delhi on September 15, 2019, decided to extend full support to this global action plan of the children. These initiatives are all welcome for the future of this planet and humanity at large.

There were three years of long negotiation leading up to the Copenhagen Summit and yet little seems to have been achieved to bring about an equitable global agreement. The so-called Annex I countries, the rich and developed countries who are the biggest polluters, are already going back on the Kyoto Protocol and the UNO Framework convention on climate change, which makes a distinction between the worst polluters and those who need the right to development.

The developed countries are wary of legally binding targets. They want to take only unilateral action. There lies the crux of the situation. It is because of this reason "Global Emission levels have increased by 14. 6 per cent between 1990 and 2006. What is in evidence is an attempt by the industrialised countries to gang up and commit less contribution and action on their part while asking the developing world, in particular India and China, to do more by way of emission reduction and targets."[17]

---

17   India Today. December 21, 2009

Therefore, we stand now where two roads diverge. But unlike the road in Robert Frost's familiar roads, they are not equally fair. The road we have been travelling is deceptively easy, a smooth superhighway on which we progress with great speed but at the end of which lies disaster. Whereas, the other road, less travelled by, offers our last chance to reach a safe destination that ensures the preservation of this earth.

We landed at the Copenhagen Global Climate Summit at this juncture. In spite of the collective wisdom of 192 leaders at the Summit on December 18, 2009, nothing tangible could be achieved. What was achieved was a mere statement of intent rather than an enforceable action plan. Copenhagen, in many ways, was doomed to failure from the very start. It was the summit in which the so-called Annex I nations under the Kyoto Protocol were to commit higher and legally binding cuts. These were to cover the second commitment period that was to be from 2012 to 2016. But under the Protocol itself, most of the nations failed to fulfil their targets in the first commitment period of 2005 to 2012 in which they were to cut down their Greenhouse Gas (GHG) emissions to an average 5 percent less than 1990 levels. However, during the period, since the UNO France World convention on climate change was signed in 1992 at the Earth Summit in Rio, the world's GHG emission levels have risen by as much as 30 percent.

The IPCC (Inter-Governmental Panel on Climate Change) stated that if global temperatures had to be prevented from rising beyond the danger mark of additional 2 degrees Celsius, the developed nations have to cut their emissions between 25 to 40 per cent below 1990 levels by 2020. However, what most countries are willing to concede would amount to barely 5 to 17 per cent of that amount. The UNFCC (United Nations Framework Convention on Climate Change) had estimated that to meet the mitigation and adaptation needs for developing countries, the advanced countries should offer at least 400 billion dollars a year.

However, the developed countries should offer at least 40 billion dollars to be directed to the least developing countries. "Not surprising when you think of the Kyoto Protocol, 1991, which was negotiated by Al Gore, the then Vice President of America, was rejected 95–0 by the Senate of the USA Congress resulting in one of the many inconvenient truths about America."[18]

The USA refused to do the needful for climate action spread like a virus across Europe, which has also toned down the big pledges they had originally made. Initially, Europe talked about cutting emission levels drastically, as much as 5 percent by 2050. That is now reduced to a modest 20 percent by 2030 if the USA agrees to do likewise. The main reason is that Europe does not want to lose its competitive edge to its rival, the USA, by introducing cuts which may result in high cost of production. This is because, renewable energy as compared to fossil fuels costs a lot more in the short term that make it an unviable option.

Another serious blow to the climate action negotiations was the economic meltdown and the ongoing recession. Job security has become the number one priority. Since the developed countries want to bring down their unemployment rates, they are not at all willing to make drastic changes in the economy that climate action measures demand.

Meanwhile, the developed countries made an effort to break the unity of the Group 77 countries by offering finance to the more needy ones, especially small islands in Asia and the Pacific which are under threat because of climate change. So a new Fund for Reducing Emissions from Deforestation and Forest Degradation was floated that would help and compensate countries like Brazil and Indonesia for preserving their forests instead of felling them to maintain the fragile ecosystem.

If the nations fix a cap of global warming at 2-degree Celsius above pre-industrial levels, the cornerstone goal of Paris Climate Deal, 2015, the

---

18 India Today. December 21, 2009.

seas will rise by half-a-metre according to a draft prepared by the IPCC. However, in a world today where efforts to curb the GHG emissions fall short of the mark, we will see an increase closer to a metre, which will be enough to cause havoc in many coastal megacities and render many small islands uninhabitable. Some small islands in the Pacific and the Indian Ocean are just one or two metres above sea level. Carlos Fuller, a leading climate negotiator for the Association of Small Islands States, told AFP: "A 1.2-metre rise would totally submerge three small States."[19]

From Australia to Asia, Africa to Europe and then to America, the refrain of those who observed a one-day strike on 20th September 2019 worldwide was that their future should be taken care of. Unfortunately, it is not the common man who is ultimately the arbiter of the planet's destiny but the people in power in the whole world. Sadly, self-interest guides the politics of nations when actions are needed to cope with the emerging situation.

However, not all is lost. Meanwhile, some countries are getting ahead of the problem by moving vulnerable populations. Recently, Indonesia announced that it would relocate its capital from Jakarta to Borneo. Vietnam, on its part, is engineering an exodus from parts of the Mekong Delta to higher ground.

Local government in Florida and Louisiana have given incentives to move people from flood-prone areas and Britain has already earmarked at least one vulnerable village in Wales to be decommissioned. The message is wide and clear that rising sea levels are affecting the rich and the poor, the developed and the developing countries alike. Some are taking an engineering approach. New York, for example, has a plan likely to cost billions of dollars to protect parts of the city inundated in 2012 by hurricanes. The recently held Madrid Global Climate Conference, better known as COP 25, came to a close on 13 December

---

19 Assam Tribune, September 22, 2019.

2019 after over two-week-long deliberations without producing any tangible outcome. Of late, these endless talks have become the butt of jokes, devoid of any substance and reduced to mere polemics. Whatever has emerged from these talks is mere eyewash as the nations will have their own National Climate Pledges (NCP) separately instead of uniform legally binding norms, which the nations are not likely to agree to implement. Moreover, the CDM is not properly spelt out at the conference, and the proposed Climate Fund is not yet ready to which the developing countries, particularly the needy ones, can have easy access. All these hurdles have to be overcome; only then can the Clean Development Mechanism materialise. However, all these measures will have to be duly mandated by the next COP 26 Summit and those will have to be subsequently ratified by the Parliament/Congresses of member nations. Till then let us wait and see what will happen.

Therefore, at the moment, the issue is not about economics, politics or finance but rather it is the issue of maintaining the ecosystem of the planet. We have come far ahead of the pre-industrialised world. There has been tremendous progress in science and technology since then. But the point is how to utilise the progress of science and technology for further betterment of the human race. We all know that we have limited resources in this universe. But we must put these limited resources to proper use and not to subserve the interests of the greedy few. Otherwise, there may be an ecological imbalance affecting the very fabric of human life. Thus, the climate change movement is not merely an economic movement for more green funds or more carbon credits alone, but it must be a social movement on the part of the people around the world to arise and awaken and to comprehend the looming danger of climate change by curbing emissions in whatever way possible. We are, after all, among all other animals, wise beings capable of maintaining a proper balance between men and other animals as an integral part of nature. This balance must not be upset for the well-being of the people and the planet we live in. How to execute an all comprehensive climate deal in a meaningful way is the main question before us in this troubled world.

CHAPTER 4

THE WORLDWIDE PROBLEM OF TERRORISM

Terrorism is a much talked about word but bereft of a full connotation, defying a solution. Nations of the world have utterly failed to define terrorism fully and comprehensively. As a matter of fact, terrorism is like unprovoked aggression against an individual, community or even against the state as well as against the time-honoured established law of the land and authority of government. It is not only against the state, its people or government established by law but also against the civilisation and culture of the land. Therefore, an act of terror may be defined as a heinous act committed in defiance of all norms, laws and authority established under the constitution and rule of law. So governments of all nations of the world have enacted laws banning terrorism in any form or manifestation.

What appears to be absurd to think is that at the beginning of the Ronald Reagan and H. W Bush administration, there was considered to be a perceived threat from the third world. I call it perceived because it was highly illogical and unreasonable to think of aggression committed by a country belonging to a third world, particularly after the disintegration of the Soviet Union. However, Bush's reason was the growing technological sophistication of the third world countries and this realisation loomed like a shadow over the American administration.

It was, however, made clear later on that their main concern was not the Russians, rather what they called the radical nationalism, meaning thereby, independent nationalism not under US control, for which intervention forces were considered very crucial.[20]

Hans Morgenthau, the founder of realist theory in international affairs, developed the view that the USA has a transcendent purpose to establish peace and freedom at home and indeed everywhere. Since the area within which the USA must defend and promote this purpose, the idea became known worldwide. This doctrine, if you can at all call it a doctrine, may be suicidal or may even stretch itself to eventually become an instrument of terrorism if it is not carefully and thoughtfully implemented. This may well be the case in Iraq, Libya, Syria, Cuba or anywhere else. Any nation should be careful in having recourse to force because the use of force as a means of settling international issues may have various ramifications that cannot be easily foretold or anticipated.

Some nations may attack other nations in the name of saving democracy or under the guise of making it safe for freedom and democracy. No doubt, these are altruistic principles. But then, in realising these principles, if there is too much of human sacrifice, one cannot agree to those methods of realising these noble principles.

There might be civilising missions in some underdeveloped countries that are not for civilising as such but for ulterior motives to gain power and pelf or with an eye to extend sway or create a vast sphere of influence.

Aggression is more serious and heinous than even terrorism. Terrorism thrives in a limited area without international ramifications. It may not spread worldwide. However, if it is not nipped in the bud, it may appeal to others and many will fall prey to acts of terror as an adventure. This does not mean that we should accept it as a matter of

---

20 Op. Cit Noam Chomsky: *Who rules the world?* National Security Strategy of the USA White House, March, 1990.

fact or way of life. We should condemn it in any form in any part of the globe.

There cannot be any kind of legitimacy of terrorism. People or communities may have grievances against certain people or against the government, but these grievances should be articulated in a constructive and democratic manner so that there is no disruption in day-to-day life. Therefore, terrorism cannot be accepted as a way of life by the people. However, it is a pity that so far, nations have failed to arrive at a consensus on the vital aspect of a foolproof definition of terrorism. As I have said earlier, aggression is more serious and heinous than terrorism because it encompasses activities that adversely affect the sovereign nations and their peoples.

Aggression has been defined but not exhaustively. The UNO General Assembly on December 14, 1974, adopted a definition on which political experts of the UNO and the former League of Nations has worked since 1923.

The first principle is aggression or the use of armed forces by a state against the sovereignty, territorial integrity or political independence of another state or in any other manner inconsistent with the charter of the UNO. Secondly, the first use of armed forces by a state in contravention of the charter of the UNO shall constitute a prima facie evidence of an act of aggression. Although, the Security Council may in conformity with the charter conclude that aggression had been committed. However, it would not be justified in the light of other relevant circumstances; including the fact that the acts concerned or their consequences were not of sufficient gravity.

The new definition lists various acts of aggression such as invasion, occupation, bombardment or blockade. There are events in history that are unparalleled; the invasion of South Vietnam was such an event in the world, which was the most destructive and inhuman, leaving millions dead and a cluster of four countries devastated with some of the most lethal carcinogens used to destroy ground cover and food crops. Though initially the attack was directed against South Vietnam, it soon spread to North Vietnam and then to the far-flung peasant societies of Laos and Cambodia.

The then President of America, John F. Kennedy, valiantly declared in no uncertain terms: "For we are opposed around the world by a monolithic and ruthless conspiracy that relies primarily on covert means for expanding its sphere of influence on infiltration instead of invasion, on subversion instead of elections, on intimidation instead of free choice, on guerrillas by night instead of armies by day."[21] If that conspiracy achieved its end in Laos and Vietnam, the gates will be opened wide. He also cautioned that the complacent, self-indulgent, soft societies are about to be swept away with the debris of history, only the strong can possibly survive.

Iraq was another case that was ill-conceived and ill-perceived. Both George W. Bush and Tony Blair proudly declared that the President of Iraq, Saddam Hussein, would go on producing weapons of mass destruction. So to resist it, in the name of saving democracy from authoritarian hands, war was declared and after the war was over, the UNO team did not find any trace of weapons of mass destruction. So the outcry was proved in vain and America's defeat was in sight. In the case of Vietnam, the same was true. War is, therefore, counterproductive since it leaves a trail of destructions behind.

A close analysis of American decline proves that China plays a dominant role in it, as has been true for the last fifty to sixty years. This decline may be traced back to the close of the Second World War when the USA possessed half of the wealth of the world. Long back, policy

---

21 John F. Kennedy as quoted by Thomas Paterson, Fixation with Cuba, Missile crisis.

planners of America were aware of the huge disparity of power vis-à-vis other nations of the world. The seminal basic viewpoint is spelt out admirably in a major white paper in 1948. This was done by one of the architects of the New World Order of the day, the Chairman of the State Department's policy planning staff, statesman and scholar, George F. Kennan. According to him, the central policy goal of the USA should be to maintain the position of disparity that separated its enormous wealth from the poverty of others to achieve that end. "We should cease to talk about vague and unreal objectives such as human rights, the raising of the living standards, and democratisation. The day is not far off when we are going to have to deal in straight power concepts. The less we are then hampered by idealistic slogans, the better."[22]

It is amusing to note that Dr Henry Kissinger formulated a rather absurd dictum: 'A region that falls out of USA control can become a virus that would spread contagion, including others to follow the same path.' In the meanwhile, the USA has lost the goodwill of MENA countries. For the first time in five hundred years, South America has taken steps to free itself from Western domination. The region has slowly moved for integration and harmonious development after being ruled for centuries by mostly European elites, tiny islands of wealth in a sea of poverty, disease and deprivation. These poor underdeveloped nations freed themselves of all military bases and IMF controls. A newly formed organisation, the Community of Latin American and Caribbean States (CELAC) includes all countries of the hemisphere apart from the USA and Canada. It is surely an American loss in this vital region.

Another development that has caused unease is the Arab Spring, which was considered as ominous for the USA, as this region is likely to slip away from the American sphere of influence. As far as American policy is concerned, the US generally favoured the rule of dictators instead of democratic leaders of doubtful integrity.

---

22 Noam Chomsky: Power and Prospects (2015), p – 220.

Sometimes, these terrorist attacks were mind-blowing as it happened in Beirut in 1983 when a double suicide bomb attack was launched on the barracks occupied by USA marines and French paratroopers, killing 241 marines and 58 paratroopers together with a sweeping attack on the USA embassy in Beirut that killed 63 people. For this attack, America blamed Imad Mughniyeh, the founder of Lebanon's Islamic Jihad organisation, who was also later eliminated.

Another heinous attack worth mentioning was, "the 1982 Israeli invasion of Lebanon which killed some twenty thousand people and devastated the southern part of the country, leaving Beirut in ruins. Later on, it was called off by the then President of America, Ronald Reagan, when the international protests became too intense to ignore."[23]

Another hot spot of global attention is the Israeli settlements. Recently the UNO regrets the new UNO position on these settlements. The UNO Secretary-General, Antonio Guterres, has expressed regret over the announcement made by the Trump administration that it no longer believes that the Israeli Settlements in the Palestinian territories are illegal. The UNO chief's spokesperson Stephane Dujarric told reporters that he said, "I can say for my part our position remains unchanged."

In a major policy shift, USA Secretary of State Mike Pompeo announced on 18th November 2019, that the USA no longer believes the Israeli settlements in Palestinian territories are illegal, asserting that previous arguments that such structures were inconsistent with international law have not helped the peace process at all. Pompeo said that the USA recognises the legal contention that individual settlements must depend upon an assessment of specific facts and circumstances on the ground.

---

23   Marines in Lebanon. New York Times. 30 September, 1982.

However, Dujarric said, as far as the UNO is concerned, "We remain guided by relevant Security Council resolutions. We remain committed to supporting the Palestinians and Israelis to achieve lasting and durable peace based on these resolutions."

The UNO Security Council Resolution 2334 reaffirmed in 2016 that Israeli's establishment of settlements on Palestinian land occupied since the 1967 war has no legal validity and constitutes a flagrant violation of international law and a major obstacle to the vision of two states living side by side in peace and security within internationally recognised borders.

The illegality of the settlements was later affirmed by the International Court of Justice. It had been recognised by Israel's highest legal authorities and government officials in late 1967 when the Settlement Projects were beginning. The criminal enterprise included the vast expansion and annexation of Greater Jerusalem, in explicit violation of repeated Security Council orders.[24]

Earlier, in a press briefing in Geneva, spokesperson for the office of the High Commissioner of Human Rights, Rupert Colville, told reporters that a change in the policy of one member state did not modify the existing international law nor its interpretation by the International Court of Justice and the UNO Security Council resolutions.

It may be mentioned that the 26th November 2008 Mumbai attack was the deadliest terror attack in Indian history in which 166 people were killed and another 300 injured caused by ten heavily armed terrorists from Pakistan.

Recently, Acting Assistant Secretary of State for South and Central Asia, Alice Wells, said, "Today, 26 November 2019, on the 11th anniversary of the attack, we remember the victims of the Mumbai attack and stand

---

24 Verdict of International Court of Justice, 30th January, 2004. The Accidental Empire: Israel and the birth of Settlements (1967 – 77). Gershom Gorenberg.

with their families in demanding that those responsible for this heinous act face justice."[25]

During the 74th session of the UNO General Assembly, 27 September 2019, the Prime Minister of India, Narendra Modi, while addressing the session said, "We believe that not for any single country but for the entire world and humanity it must be said that terrorism dents the very avowed principles on the basis of which the UNO was established."[26]

At the moment, the biggest threat to humankind is the ICBM (inter-continental ballistic missiles). The world will be a better place to live in when the production of these weapons ceases and nations of the world unanimously decide to ban the weapons fully and irrevocably. These weapons of mass destruction and terrorism in any form should be equally banned throughout the world.

---

25 The statement of Alice Wells, the Acting Secretary of State of USA for South and Central Asia. 26th November, 2019.

26 Assam Tribune, 28 September, 2019.

CHAPTER 5

TRADE WAR: DIVISIVE POLITICS AT WORK

Good and well thought out economic policies have the power to change the lives of the poor. Governments should adopt sound policies that help countries grow and ensure that the growth is equitably shared. Even privatisation may help here and there – that is selling off government monopolies to private enterprises – but only if it helps companies become much more efficient and capable and results in lower prices for consumers. This may happen if the markets are competitive. Good economies will not do if there is no good politics and good policies. Take for instance the IMF (International Monetary Fund). Decisions are sometimes made based on ideology or bad economies tempered by what we may call special interest. This is bad policy. There should be a set of sound rules to govern decisions that must reflect social justice and well-being. While doing so, decisions must be arrived at democratically, so that governing bodies and authorities must ensure the aspirations for whom these decisions are taken are beneficial.

As for the IMF, it has a dominant role to play in inter-nation assistances. It reviews each recipient's macro-economic fundamentals to ensure whether the country in question is living within means. No doubt, a country can live beyond its means by borrowing. But then a day may come when there is an economic crisis or downturn. The IMF is very much concerned about inflation as it may eat into the profits of the creditors, equally affecting the consumers. This happens because the deficits must be covered by printing more currency, which will have a chain of reaction.

In Far East Asia, the developing countries opened their economies to the outside world gradually and cautiously. They fully took advantage of globalisation to expand their exports and ensure faster growth. They lessened the trade protective barriers carefully. As a result, new enterprises were created giving rise to numerous job opportunities. Even China did not lag behind. It did not close its doors. It removed trade barriers after opening its markets. As a result, its economy flourished.

The Western countries pushed trade liberalisation for the products they exported, but at the same time, they continued to protect those sectors in which competition from developing countries might have threatened their economy.

During the Uruguay Round negotiations, trade services were introduced. In the end, markets even opened mainly for services and information technology. However, maritime and construction services were excluded in which developing countries would have gained a foothold.

Investment in a country, whether developed or developing, creates growth, which is good for the receiving country. Foreign direct investment is not one of the three main pillars of the Washington Consensus, but it definitely is a key part of the new globalisation. According to the Washington Consensus, growth occurs through liberalisation, privatisation and macro stability and is supposed to create a climate of investment. Foreign business brings with it technical know-how and access to foreign markets, giving rise to new employment opportunities. Foreign companies who have access to sources of finance are congenial for developing countries where local financial institutions are weak. Foreign direct investment has played a crucial role in many countries of the developing world; however, the successful development stories of Singapore, Malaysia and China can be attributed to other factors.

When Walmart comes to a community, there are often strong protests from local firms who fear rightly that they will be displaced. Local enterprises worry that they will not be able to compete with Walmart, which has huge buying power. These concerns are much more true and pronounced in developing countries. Although such concerns are natural, one has to have a perspective. The reason why Walmart is successful is that it provides goods to the community at lower prices. More efficient delivery of goods and services to the economically backward within the developing countries is more important considering the standard of living of the people.

Sometimes, the IMF behaves like a political institution. This was the case when Boris Yeltsin was in power. During these times, basic economic principles were compromised. Even in the heyday of very high prices, Russia was barely able to make its budget balanced. It was not wise enough in putting money aside for the likelihood of a rainy day. So what is needed is an investment-friendly environment. This means proper actions must be initiated at all levels of the government. A plethora of rules and regulations at all levels makes it difficult to establish new businesses. Unavailability of land may be an obstacle just as lack of finance. Privatisation does little good if local governments squeeze firms so hard that they have no incentive to invest. The best course is to provide a federal structure that provides compatible incentives at all levels. It may also happen that policies aimed at curtailing abuses at lower levels of government can themselves be abused.

It is surmised that India may be one of the big winners from the USA–China trade war according to Credit Suisse Survey of the 100 companies with global sales of $1 trillion. USA Commerce Secretary Wilbur Ross said in New Delhi during the India Economic Summit on 3 October 2019, that India has a wonderful opportunity right now to take advantage of trade discussions elsewhere. The Commerce Secretary Report says that firms in China plan to move production to Vietnam, India, Taiwan and even Mexico. The shrinking Chinese workforce is one of the main issues. It will be 50 million fewer workers by 2030.

Economists at the IMF think and worry a lot about balance of payments deficit. Such trade deficits plague different countries at different times. Such deficits are a sure sign of a problem in the offing. But as to dealing with such trade deficits, the governments often pay little attention as to how the money is being spent. If a government has a fiscal surplus, as did Thailand in the years before the 1997 crisis, then the balance of payments deficit arises from private investments exceeding private savings. If a firm in the private sector borrows a million dollars at 5% interest and invests it in something that yields 20% return, then it is not a problem for it to have borrowed the million dollars. Because the return on investment will be more than the capital cost.

It is seen that good economic policies can have the power to change the lives of the people. Globalisation should itself mean the removal of trade barriers by closer integration of national economies. It has the potential to enrich everyone in the world. There must be a mixture of good economics with politics and ethics.

"The new round of trade negotiations that was agreed to in November 2001 at Doha (Qatar) has been characterised as the development round intended not just to open up markets further but to rectify some of the imbalances of the past. The debate at Doha was far more open than in the past. The IMF and the World Bank have changed the rhetoric – there was much more talk about poverty and at the World Bank there is a sincere attempt to live up to its commitment to put the country in the driver's seat in its programmes in many countries."[27]

---

27 Stiglitz, Joseph; globalization and its discounts. Pg 215. Op.cit

The greatest challenge is not just in the IMF, the world or even the WTO but also in changing mindsets. Taking care of the prevailing environment and making sure that the deprived have a say in decision-making on issues that affect them and their fate and future are crucial and need attention. Promoting democracy side by side with fair trade is essential if the benefits of globalisation are to be reaped.

The whole field of global trade and commerce is embroiled in complexity and is time-consuming. Various issues and problems are at play. A high interest rate is good for the creditor, provided he is paid back. But workers see high interest rates as inducing an economic slowdown. For them, this means unemployment; no wonder they see the danger in a high rate of interest. For the banks or the financier who has lent his money for the long term, the real danger is inflation, which will take away or eat into his profits. In sustaining an ideal market system, the government must be proactive.

There are striking differences in the model of the market system. The German, Japanese, Swedish or the American systems have their differences and variations. Say, in Sweden, the government takes a greater role in promoting social welfare like public health, better employment, insurance and retirement benefits even more than the USA.

At the centre, an international trade war seems to be the one between the USA and China. US President Donald Trump imposed tariffs last year on billion dollars' worth of Chinese goods exported to the USA, seeking to ramp up pressure for changes in Chinese trade and investment policies. China retaliated with a tariff hike of its own. The USA's new National Security Advisor, Robert O'Brien, said that an initial trade agreement with China was still possible by the end of the year. However, the USA would not take a bad deal and would not ignore what was happening in Hong Kong.

O'Brien also said that US allies should think hard before allowing Chinese technology giant Huawei into their next generation of telecommunication network, citing surveillance concerns. He questioned: "What the Chinese are doing makes Facebook and Google look like child's play as far as collecting information on folks. Once they know the full profile of every man, woman and child in your country, how are they going to use that?"[28]

Local wars, unless diffused, can harm others, leading to global disturbances. An economic slowdown in one country can lead to a slowdown everywhere. It is a chain reaction. In 1998, the great concern was that a crisis in emerging markets might lead to a global economic meltdown.

In these situations, global collective action is desirable. There are environmental issues. Global warming caused by the highly industrialised countries' use of fossil fuels leading to GHG emissions affects those in the pre-industrial economies. The ozone layer damaged by the use of chlorofluorocarbon (CFCs) affects all. In order to cope with the international environmental issues, international conferences have been signed like the Montreal Protocol, Kyoto Protocol, 2005, etc., though much of the work on global warming remains hanging over the fire. If the developed countries are really serious about listening to the voices of the developing countries, they should establish an independent think tank that will help them in preparing a road map of development in their countries by making use of the blueprint and strategies as chalked out by the members of the think tank. It will be immensely helpful for developing countries.

Another area in which the developing countries are in a fix is the risk in management. Today, countries around the world face enormous risks from the volatility of exchange rates. Therefore, developing

---

28 Assam Tribune, November 25, 2019.

countries must be made to learn to manage risks by buying insurance against fluctuations in the international capital markets. Unfortunately, today the developing countries can buy insurance for only short-term fluctuations. The developed countries are in a much better position to handle such risks. They should step in and develop such insurance markets.

Global public goods should normally be exempt from too much of bureaucracy. Besides, aid money should be freed from domestic politics, which hampers development in developing countries that receive the aid money. Issuing special drawing rights in favour of recipient countries to prevent themselves from the vicissitudes of the international markets is definitely a safe safeguard. It will maintain the stability of the global economy and at the same time save the poor economies. In Asia, a variety of models worked well. This is true of Malaysia, S. Korea, China and Taiwan.

As regards the Beijing vis-à-vis Washington Consensus at Davos back in 2011, it captured the imagination that China would overtake the USA not only in the economy but also as a leading economic model. The USA did not take any action after the meltdown even after three years, which led to the global financial crisis. This was largely due to the bickering between the Democrats and the Republicans. During the relevant period, China's growth was double-digit when the USA did not grow well. Therefore, the consensus implied that many countries saw the virtues of an active authoritarian economy replacing the old Washington Consensus in support of free markets, trade and politics. The new theme was the rise of state capitalism. This was the talk of the European and American political and business elites, but not in emerging nations.[29]

---

29 Sharma, Ruchir, The Rise and Fall of Nations

In India, however, the talk in the business circles was not about the Beijing consensus but about the rising middle class who was instrumental in decision-making at various levels. This seems to be the product of an over-indulged bureaucracy and classic symptom of state capitalism. The resilience of China's economy and the increasingly popular idea that the state could command strong economic growth had a huge impact on investors' psychology. China's largest oil company, Petro China, having displaced Exxon Mobil was further proof that China's command economy could be more profitable than America's market economy.

When spending becomes a problem, the whole economy will be poorer one day. Subsidisation is a bottleneck for growth. Scandals ruin public services and institutions. The worst possible sign comes when a relatively fat state is getting fatter. The French government spends an annual sum equal to 57% of the GDP, more than any other nation of the world. Other wealthy countries in which state spending dominates the economy, amounting to the bulk of the GDP, are Sweden, Finland, Belgium, Denmark and Italy.

The whole edifice of state authority is weak.

Since the early 1980s, the output of private firms in China has risen by 300 times, five times faster than state companies according to a Deutsche Bank piece of research. As a result, the share of state companies of GDP has fallen from 70% to 30%. Journalist and author Evan Osnos writes in the *Age of Ambition* that between 1993–2005, the Chinese state companies eliminated 73 million jobs; all those workers were to find other sources of income. Therefore, China's successes were less a tribute to command capitalism than to Beijing's steady free-market reform.[30]

---

30   Rajan, Raghuram, Fault Lines. Op.cit.

A few words about Rajan: Rajan, besides being the Ex-Governor of RBI, is a celebrated economist known internationally for his economic ideas and principles. He traces in his book, how mismanaged and ill-conceived

The average state banks controlled 32% of all banking assets in the twenty largest emerging nations. This figure is 40% in Thailand, Indonesia, Brazil and China. It is 50% or more in Taiwan, Hungary, Russia, Malaysia and 70% in India. In contrast, the private banks in India tend to be independent not only of the state but also of control by large tycoons, which is quite unusual in the emerging world.

George Clemenceau, an early 20th century President, described France as a very fertile country: "You plant bureaucrats and taxes grow." Greece used to be one of the countries where state spending accounted for half of the GDP, but since the crisis of 2008, its share of the GDP fell by 4%. Among the twenty largest emerging nations, Brazil is the biggest spender with 41% of the GDP, Argentina and Poland with 40% and Russia and Turkey are 5% above the norm ($12000 per capita income). In Taiwan and South Korea, government spending accounts for a 22% share of the economy. Even the rich Asian countries like Japan have been slow to build a welfare state. Only 30% of Asia's population is covered by a pension plan compared to more than 90% in Europe. Mexico collects taxes equal to about 14% of the GDP, which is quite low for a middle-class country. Mexico spends only 0.6% of the GDP on the military, while Nigeria 0.5%. In Pakistan, a nation of 150 million people, fewer than four million people are registered with the tax authority, while less than one million actually pay taxes.

---

economic policies can ruin the economy of a country. A market economy can transform a backward economy, provided it is properly monitored and regulated. An efficient banking system can do a lot for the development of the economy of a country. In his words, "Finance is not everything. Finance, if it is mismanaged may lead to ruin. All the financial institutions, including banks, must act in tandem with utmost care, only then there will be no shutdowns in an economy."

Nonetheless, there are periodic market failures like periodic market slumps, recessions and depressions that have brought a bad name for capitalism during the last two hundred years.

Adam Smith himself was aware of the limitations of the market induced by imperfect competition. He was more aware of the social and political context in which all economies will have to function. Social cohesion is essential if an economy is to function properly. Urban violence in Latin America and civil disorder in Africa create environments that are a dis-incentive to investment and development.

"Opposition to globalisation in many parts of the world is not to globalisation per se, but to the new sources of funds for growth or to the new export markets but to the particular set of doctrines, the Washington Consensus policies, that the international financial institutions have imposed."[31]

Dilma Rousseff, the Ex-President of Brazil, has to say this much on market economy: "A market self-regulation is no substitute for government regulation. We should build a more balanced relationship between states and the market. We should all move to a more environmentally sustainable economic model."

---

31   Stiglitz, Joseph, Globalization and its Discontents. Op.cit.

Stiglitz, Joseph was a former Chief Economist at the World Bank and was Chairman of then President of America, Bill Clinton's Council of Economic Advisors. He is presently Professor of finance and Economics at the Columbia University. He was awarded the Nobel Prize for Economics in 2001.

He argues that the West has seriously mismanaged the process of privatization, liberalization and following the advice of the World Bank and IMF. Third World countries and farmer communist states are actually worse off now than they were before. He is, however, not against globalization, but deals with the difficult and complex realities of the world.

It seems that sometimes globalisation is attacked because it undermines traditional values. Development induced by globalisation results in rapid urbanisation undermining traditional rural societies. At times, it becomes a threat to cultural identity and norms. In small towns and semi-urban areas, it kills small business or retailers and their communities.

In the West, the largest gains in productivity are associated with privatisation, with corporatisation imposing hard budget and commercial practices but are yet under active state control. Rapid capital market liberalisation without the accompanying regulation can be very dangerous. The developing and poor countries should enact bankruptcy and social security laws to act as a cushion in case of crises. Therefore, nations need a multipronged strategy of reform without which true development cannot take place. The paradigm of development is not helping a few people to get rich or for creating an island of affluence in a sea of poverty.

CHAPTER 6

THE THREAT OF NUCLEAR WAR

The threat of a possible nuclear war and its dark clouds are still looming menacingly on the horizon of the world. No one knows who will attack whom. To me, the threat seems to be more now than during the Cold War period.

In the past, most of the American public and even the government perceived the threat of nuclear attack from Russia. The political history of the world has enough to show this threat perception was there. But then, was it real? Or was it that the fear was magnified so much so that it was reduced to nothing but a big fantasy? Actually, this perceived nuclear threat disappeared in 1991 after the disintegration of Soviet Russia. No nation on earth should formulate its major foreign policy based on a perceived threat because this is nothing but an illusion. The same logic was followed by the foreign policymakers of America concerning Iraq, Iran, Vietnam or even some of the Latin American countries.

Now we hear talk of another type of threat from the Arab world, usually called radical nationalism.[32]

This type of nationalism is called in American political parlance an independent nationalism not under USA control.

---

32 National Security Strategy of the USA, White House, March, 1990.

The then President of Soviet Russia, Mikhail Gorbachev, agreed to allow the re-unification of Germany with its membership of NATO. Both the then US President, George Bush, and his Secretary of State, James Baker, were good enough to promise that the NATO would never expand even one inch into East Germany. But later on, Mikhail Gorbachev was dismayed when it was made known to him that the agreement was merely a Gentleman's Agreement without any binding force.[33] Subsequently, George Bush's successor President Bill Clinton expanded NATO up to the Russian border.

It is said in Latin America that Guatemala was one of the world's worst horror places where there was a dramatic deterioration of the political, economic and social context. Attacks were directed against those who tried to defend rights under the Roland Reagan Administration. Indigenous people were dislodged from their ancestral homes overnight to make way for mining industries and those who launched social movements were criminalised or killed.[34]

More recently, existential and survival questions have cropped up because of a tug of war between China and the USA. This is ominous for mankind and for the planet we live in. One must think deeply before making any reckless, thoughtless or sweeping political, economic or strategic decisions that impact the people and nations around the world. God helps those who help themselves, the saying goes.

Recently, I was dismayed to come across an ominous message in the BBC News Report from the popular Russian President, Vladimir Putin, who said that the USA is militarising outer space.[35] This is highly dangerous, to say the least, and spells doom for the earth.

---

33   Noam Chomsky: Hopes and Prospects: 2010.

34   Luis Paiz to Noam Chomsky: 13 June, 2014.

35   BBC News Report: 5.12.2019.

Moreover, NATO, which has been so long a stabilising force for Europe and the Northern Hemisphere, is tottering because of a clash of interest among the members of the organisation. As for the USA, it asserts that it can't take the massive burden of NATO and will reduce the funding pattern to just 16% instead of the present 22% above. So, there is a simmering cold war among the members of NATO. France's President, Immanuel Macron, on his part, calls the condition of present NATO 'brain dead.' On the other hand, the President of Turkey, Recep Tayyip Erdogan, does not want NATO to cover the security of the Baltic region, which, however, some of the powerful members endorse. There is also a perceptible conflict of interest between France and Germany. The British Prime Minister, on the other hand, wants to streamline the organisation and is urging the member nations not to do anything that jeopardises the organisation.

The European Union, which is said to be one of the most promising developments of the post-World War II period, has been in doldrums because of the hard policies of austerity during recession. This action was condemned even by the economists of the IMF. In the process, democracy had been undermined as decisions were arrived at in Brussels, which were confined to a narrow circle of big bureaucracy. The executive director of Paris-based research group Europe Nova (EUROPANOVA) attributes the general disenchantment to a mode of angry impotence at the real power to shape events that were largely shifted from national leaders, who in principle, at least, are subject to democratic politics to market the institutions of the European Union and corporations quite in accordance with the neo-liberal doctrine.[36]

At the present moment, there is a persistent and vociferous opposition to the USA–UK onslaught on any part of the globe. On the front page of the *New York Times*, journalist Patrick Tyler reported that

---

36 Alison Smale and Andrew Higgins: Election results in Spain: A bitter year for leaders in Europe.

there might still be two superpowers on the planet – The USA and the World Public Opinion.[37]

What is not easily understood and intriguing is the fact that the general mission of NATO is officially changed to a mandate to protect the crucial infrastructure of the global energy system, sea lanes and pipelines, giving it a global area of operations. Therefore, under the Western revision of the so-called doctrine of responsibility to protect NATO may now also serve as an intervention force under US command.[38]

Commitment to move Ukraine out of Moscow's orbit and integrate it into the West is considered by the Russian President Putin as a direct threat to Russia's core interests.

Moreover, as per the Monroe Doctrine of 1823, the USA does not tolerate the deployment of the forces of other powerful nations in the Western Hemisphere in defiance of the above doctrine.

The intervention in the Middle East time and again gave rise to the mounting refugee crisis. No doubt, in the way of the crisis, Germany emerged as the conscience keeper of Europe, admitting about one million refugees into one of the richest countries of Europe, with a population of eighty million, whereas Lebanon, a small country, absorbed roughly 1.5 million Syrian refugees.

Now there is no other principle but only one principle that governs the world at present – national self-interest and existential concerns rule the world. Then there is the question of supremacy, which is uppermost in the conscience, in the leaders of most of the nations of the world. Undoubtedly, this is a tragedy of our times.

The saying goes that 'a spark neglected burns the house.' This possibility is true today in respect of the prevailing situation in Yemen

---

37 'A New Power in the Street'. Patrick Tyler. New York Times. 17 Feb. 2003.

38 Op.cit. Noam Chomsky: Hopes and Prospects (2010).

which has two factions, one the A M Hadi led Yemeni government and the other the movement led by Houthis, backed by Iran. The former faction is backed by Saudi Arabia. This is just a Civil War between these warring factions. Recently, after the attacks made by Houthis on Saudi Arabia's oil installations, particularly on the world's Oil Refinery Aramco, stringent sanctions were imposed by the USA against Iran. As a result, bad blood and a cold war are developing between the USA and Iran. This event, if it remains unchecked, may snowball into a major catastrophe in the future, endangering world peace.

Once, Ex-President of the USA Dwight Eisenhower warned the nation that a nuclear war was all too imminent, a war that might destroy the Northern Hemisphere. Ex-President, J F Kennedy's own judgement was that the probability of war might have been as high as 50%.[39]

Kennedy's close associate, the historian Arthur M. Schlesinger Jr., described the event as the most dangerous moment in human history.[40]

Kennedy had already declared the highest nuclear alert, short of launch DEFCON (defence readiness condition), which authorised NATO aircraft with Turkish pilots or others to take off, fly to Moscow and drop a bomb, according to Harvard University Strategic Analyst Graham Allison, writing in Foreign Affairs.[41]

However, the then Soviet President, Nikita Khrushchev, sent a message directly to Kennedy: "The missiles would be removed if the USA promised not to invade Cuba." Khrushchev considered the deployment of the missiles as a defensive move to protect his allies rather than to

---

39 Michael Dobbs: 'One minute to midnight', Kennedy, Khrushchev and Castro, on the brink of a Nuclear War. (New York: Vintage, 2008).

40 Ibid as quoted by Noam Chomsky is his work: 'Who rules the World?' page 101.

41 Graham Allison: 'The Cuban Missile Crisis: Lessons for the USA Foreign Policy Today, Foreign Affairs. August, 2012.

be a menace to the USA since it gave the appearance of equality in the nuclear balance of powers. Castro had a real fear of American possible attempt at regime change. This is amply corroborated by Sheldon Stern in his book — *The Week the World Stood Still: Inside the Secret Cuban Missile crisis: Stanford University Press, 2005.*

There is an underlying basic principle that the USA effectively owns the world by right and is by definition a force for good, despite occasional errors and misunderstandings, in principle, in which it is plainly entirely proper for the USA to deploy massive offensive force all over the world, while it is an outrage for others to make even the slightest gesture in that direction or even to think of deterring the threatened use of violence by the benign global hegemon.[42]

The above doctrine is the primary official charge even today against Iran. It might pose a deterrent to the USA and Israeli forces. That is a consideration during the circumstances for which nations go to war and freely use these weapons of mass destruction in an attempt to solve bilateral problems. There must be a way of solving mutual problems or conflicts short of the use of these deadly weapons. Nations should always make a sincere endeavour to solve their problems through bilateral dialogue, diplomacy or even mediation by a third neutral party if both sides agree to such an approach. Under such circumstances, there should always be a guiding principle of international disputes, this being the principle of give and take.

Some in the West think that Iran is the greatest threat to world peace. However, is it really so by its attitudes and deeds? It seems to be a peace-loving nation among some of the most hostile nations. It is, therefore, a Western obsession.

When it comes to action, such an action plan for a nuclear-free zone was proposed in the Non-Aligned Conference held in Tehran in

---

42 Op.cit. Noam Chomsky: 'Who rules the World?'

2013. In fact, such a proposal had been on the table for decades and was approved by the General Assembly of the UNO. There was to be an International Conference in Finland, but for reasons not known, it was abruptly called off by the then President of America, Barack Obama. Even the Euro Parliament and Arab states backed it. But nothing tangible materialised.

Very recently, on 5th December 2019, at the London NATO Summit, member nations voiced their concerns against Chinese challenges, particularly the USA. Reacting to these concerns, China's Foreign Ministry Spokeswoman, Hua Chunying, said that the growth of China's power is the growth of peaceful power and that there is not necessarily a connection between the threat and size of the country. Speaking at a regular press conference, she said the largest threat facing the world today is unilateralism and bullying actions. Even American allies have been harmed.

The two-day summit was overshadowed by bad blood with Donald Trump branding Canada's Prime Minister as two-faced after a group of allied leaders were caught on video at Buckingham Palace mocking the USA President's rambling press conferences.

NATO's Summit Declaration stressed the need for securing resilient communication, particularly 5G infrastructure. This points to the growing anxiety in NATO and the West at large about the role of Chinese companies, particularly Huawei, in building networks needed for the next generation of mobile communication.[43]

During the NATO Summit, the British Prime Minister, Boris Johnson, said that the NATO is the most enduring and successful alliance in military history and that it continues to adapt to the evolving threat that we face today. It is the cornerstone of Euro-Atlantic security and it helps to keep a billion people safe. All members of NATO must be united

---

43 AFP News. Assam Tribune, 5 December, 2019.

behind shared priorities so that NATO can adapt to the challenges ahead.

However, the French President took an opposite stand and assailed the NATO as 'brain dead' to which the USA President reacted and remarked that it was very insulting. There has been conflict among the NATO members in regard to finance of the NATO. Moreover, the Turkish President Recep Tayyip Erdogan has said that he will oppose NATO's plan for the defence of the Baltic region if it does not back Turkey over its fight against Kurdish groups that it considers terrorists. So there are simmering conflicts among the members of NATO at the moment. Time alone will reveal what will happen in future.

In this context, the cases of India and Pakistan may be considered relevant because both of them came closer to using nuclear weapons at the time of hostilities in the past, during 1965, 1971 and right up to the present crisis over Jammu and Kashmir, which still remains a bone of contention between the two countries even after 73 years after independence in 1947. Both these countries have refused to sign the Nuclear Non-Proliferation Treaty along with Israel and have received support from not only the USA but also from the Soviet Union and France as well. So there is always a looming danger of using nuclear weapons in the event of hostilities. There must be a universal nuclear deterrence mechanism sponsored by the UNO, so that nations cannot, under any circumstances, use nuclear warheads.

CHAPTER 7

BALANCE OF POWER

Until modern times, every super state sprang into a greater height of power and glory like a single sun surrounded by smaller satellites but forming no constellation with other states. Usually, there was one state dominant in each civilisation. If another state rose into prominence and domination, the issue was fought out in order to outsmart one another. It happened in the past as between Rome and Carthage. When this phase passed off at the dawn of the modern world, a number of great power-states appeared in the horizon during the Western Civilisation. The conflicts between these states were never settled by the imperial supremacy of any nation. Spain might rise to greatness for a time. So also, France became the dominant power of a continent. England too became an undisputed maritime power in the empire. But the power could not control the rest, however much it might inspire them with its fears. The sources of power and the area of civilisation were too extensive to allow force play in the presence of a plurality of independent powers.

Even after the great attempt of Napoleon to restore the principle of hegemony, the Concert of Europe was brought into being because the power-standing of the states changed from time to time. The very concept of Concert disappeared or evaporated in the air, requiring some sort of a balance of power. Such was the European situation on the eve of World War I. As a result, the powers of Europe penetrated into the whole world. The British Empire spread far and wide, spreading over five continents. France brought under its control a large African territory, besides possession in other parts of the world. Russia also held sway over two continents. The great new emerging power of the USA abandoned an exclusively American policy to share the problems of a world system. Lastly, Japan adopting economic civilisation as the methods of imperialism added another feeder to world power.

The external history of European states, especially since the Franco-Prussian war, presents a curious spectacle of shifting relationships based on the balance of power equations. However, at the same time, every state seeks to augment its military and naval power apart from its allies for no one really trusts the fragile balance of power. The failure to control power was in part due to the discrimination of external from internal affairs, which in turn, was a consequence of the traditional doctrine of state sovereignty. The real power, in the last resort, is the expression of the character and the resources of its people. It is not a power that lies dormant except in the hour of conflict with an opponent power. It is exerted in and through all the activities, both economic and cultural, of the people. The power of Spain declined because she ceased to display this inner vitality as she failed to keep abreast with other states in respect of culture. As a result, her trade and wealth declined. The power of England increased because the energy of her people enabled her to reap the advantages of her geographical position and her mineral resources in an age that gave new value to both. It was not because she waged a successful war against France and other states. The power of the US, based on the enterprise with which her citizens developed the vast resources of a new continent, has given her a foremost place among the states of the world.

In the modern world, an empire has to pass into voluntary cooperation and the world power must increasingly abate the exercise of force if it is to survive at all. Free exploitation gives rise to monopoly rights, concessions and other privileges and these, in turn, become difficult to maintain and sustain within the order of the world economies.

It seems world powers unite across the lines of civilization and culture. Culturally, England belongs to Europe, but politically it is united with countries that belong to other systems. Say with Canada, which is geographically and economically and in less measure culturally, a part of America or with India, which is the heart of the Oriental World. The eccentricity of the states, and civilisations, which marks the extension of world power, confounds the polity of force and robs it of significance. This becomes more apparent as democracy develops within the world power itself.[44]

The bedrock of the balance of power is the four freedoms as developed by the former President of the USA, D. Roosevelt, which may be summarised as under:

1. Freedom of speech and expression everywhere in the world.

2. Freedom of every person to worship God in his own way, everywhere in the world.

3. Freedom from want, which, translated into word form means economic understanding, which will secure to every nation a healthy and peaceful life for its inhabitants everywhere in the world.

4. Freedom from fear, which translated into word form means a worldwide reduction of armaments to such a point that a country cannot commit an act of aggression against any neighbour anywhere in the world.[45]

When Winston Churchill wrote about the balance of power in his book *The Second World War: The Gathering Storm*, as the

---

44 R.M. MacIver: The Modern State.

45 Roosevelt, the Ex-President of the USA

wonderful tradition of British foreign policy, it was clear that he had in mind balance of power as forever discredited and sought legal and institutional arrangement through the League of Nations; we have a different perception of the balance of power.[46]

Whenever there is a rough equilibrium of power between various nations, we say there is a balance of power. However, when we use it in relation to a power or nation, we usually mean that it has a superior or preponderance of power. From the behaviour of nations, we find that nations have often preferred preponderance, not equilibrium of power. So nations seeking the balance of power may refer to a situation in which powers seek a condition of (disequilibrium) and not of equilibrium of power. As such, curiously enough, balance of power sometimes means equilibrium or disequilibrium. The truth of the matter is that states are interested only in a balance that is in their favour. The balance desired is one that neutralises other states, leaving aside the home state free to be the deciding force and the deciding voice in the international relations.

The balance is the pivot of the concept of balance of power. But it requires high acumen to perform the role of a successful balance, as England played during the 19th century because of its unchallenged supremacy and mastery over the seas. But balance of power does not work well today as there is no balancer to effect the balance between the powers. After World War II, no state or group of states has been a real balance. However, after the disintegration of the Soviet Union and the Cold War, nations have more or less ceased to talk about balance. They are rather lukewarm in their approach to this idea. The balance of power seems to have disappeared and simply because of that, can we say that there is a breakdown of the balance itself?

---

46 Winston Churchill: The Second World War: The Gathering Storm.

If one takes it for granted that balance of power is a permanent feature in international politics, as its protagonists believe, the balancer must not disappear at all. The emergence of non-aligned nations in the post-war period is considered to have given rise to a new type of balancer. In the wake of the emergence of this factor, the balance of power wielded by the small and big nations is said to help prevent aggression and it is often defended on the ground that it has the capacity to achieve durable peace.

Moreover, balance of power is based on the contention that small states cannot individually strike a balance vis-à-vis the great powers and the only course open to the struggle for power can help them in their quest for security. However, after the end of the Cold War, there is a perceptible dilution of rivalry among superpowers. It has radically changed the international power scenario, keeping the concept of balance of power in cold storage at least for the time being. But then, one must not rush to the conclusion that it has become outdated. It may still be relevant, though its relevance would largely depend upon how far its technique is modified to fit in well with the changed circumstances. It cannot work in old conditions obtained in the 18th or 19th-century world. Thus, the solution of the problem of proper balance lies in seeking an alternative to it or a new mechanism for its operation.

CHAPTER 8

NATIONALISM: REAL OR FICTION

A nation needs territory, but it is not just equal to its territory. Not in all nations is nationalism alike. An organically evolved nation is the collective consciousness of a people with a shared history of values and ideals. The mutually contrasting examples of the USA and Israel may be considered in this context. The USA is said to be a nation of immigrants. It is a less organically and more artificially evolved nation on earth. National consciousness may pervade in a people well-organised and disciplined even without well-demarcated territory, as in the case of Israel before 1948. The Jewish people are spread around the world for over two thousand years. They thrived even without a National Home for these years. Israeli nationalism is decidedly racial and a legacy of the history of the hoary past.

The Vedas speak of *Rastra* (state). In the *Vishnu Purana*, *Brahmapurana* and *Murkandaya Purana*, Greater India was known as *Bharatvarsha*. The *Puranas* talked of spiritualism as the soul of Bharat. Tagore advised his fellow Indians to study Swami Vivekananda to know the true spirit of India. Even Nehru was of the opinion that Swami Vivekananda was one of the great founders of the national movement who inspired the freedom fighters. Even Aurobindo and Subramanya Bharti were deeply inspired by Vivekananda. Chakravarty Raja Gopalachari also shared the same view.[47]

---

47 Chakravarty Raja Gopalachari (1879 – 1972) was the first and last Governor General of India. He was the Chief Minister of Madras, now Tamil Nadu

Justice Barucha speaking for himself and Justice Ahmed said, "Hinduism is a tolerant faith. It is that tolerance that has enabled Islam, Christianity, Zoroastrianism, Judaism, Buddhism, Jainism, Sikhism and other religions find shelter and support upon this land."[48]

The sense of nationality, therefore, is the sense of community, which under historical conditions of a particular social epoch, has possessed or still seeks expression through the mechanism and unity of the state. The sense of nationality is itself definite, strong and moving, more so than the mere pride and glory of egoism so that men are aroused by its name and thought to deep stirrings of devotion, sacrifice or even worship. This is soul unity. It is because of this realisation, in spite of differences in their manners of thought and life and belonging to different worlds in their daily interests, that they continue to belong to the same nation and feel a sense of oneness that in the time of crisis supersedes all obvious differences transcending all class differences. These differences when real are typical rather than universal. Many Englishmen are not typical English in physical features or in the mode of thought or behaviour, yet they are conscious of their nationality. Surely, these subtle similarities are not the decisive conditions of our modern civilisation.

Ashoka's use of *Jambudipa* for a vast region in the third century BC of the Kalinga rulers' reference to Bharata in the same century are the first indications of the consciousness of a geographically definable territory in which similar cultured conditions prevailed.

The tribes of the Cesarian Gaul are themselves the product of invasion and fusion. They are unities born out of the endless process

---

(1937–39) and Governor of West Bengal (1956–57) Minister without portfolio, Union Cabinet. He was a shrewd and serious political thinker and one of the founders of the Swatantra party.

48 Op. cit. S Gurumurthy. Outlook. February 5, 2018.

of social assimilation. The inner ground of their loyalty is not a race, but felt community of place, custom, tradition and authority and the common lot and fortune, which thereon they depend. The sense of nationality has a content more pervasive and more real than the conception of social unity that preceded it. It belongs to a stage where social consciousness is different and diffused through the various classes of society.

It is very like the 'common consciousness of a common end' as depicted by T H Green.[49] To him, the state is a natural growth with an ethical end. It is an embodiment of what Hegel calls the spirit. It is a product of human consciousness. He stated: "Human consciousness postulates liberty, liberty involves rights; rights demand the state."

It belongs to an era that advances to democracy and parliament, where monarchy disappears and rule of law sets in. It applies to all men, rich or poor, high and low. It is not external and it is not transferable except by a long process of assimilation. The state becomes the finality of our being and remains exalted over everybody else. It is the culmination of the people's consciousness. Though the present state may not be the most perfect and flawless one, it is still evolving and growing, there being no absolute finality in its long-conquered journey.

In his celebrated essay on liberty, J S Mill thoroughly examines the problem of the relationship between the individual on one side and the

---

49 T H Green belongs to the idealist school of philosophy that was dead against the 18th century nationalism and the 19th century empiricism and utilitarianism. He was chiefly influenced by the Greek classics, German idealism and British liberalism. He was born in 1836 and died at an early age of 46. In 1855, he joined the Ballid College teaching history, ethics, metaphysics, logic and philosophy. He was appointed Whyte Professor of Moral Philosophy in 1878.He was not a mere academician. He was a member of various commissions and an active member of the Liberal Party.

society and state on the other side. Mill felt that the over-regulation of the individual by state or society amounted to tyranny.

The individual needed protection against the society as much as against over legislation and regulation by the state. The society had the tendency of compelling the individual to conform to its own ideas and practices as rules of conduct. He believed, "The sole end for which mankind are warranted individually or collectively in interfering with the liberty of action of any other member is self-protection. The only purpose for which power can be rightfully exercised over any member of a civilised community against his will is to prevent harm to others. His own good either physical or moral is not a sufficient warrant. The only part of the conduct of anyone for which he is amenable to society is that which concerns others. In the part which merely concerns himself, the individual, his independence is of right absolute over himself, over his own body or mind, the individual is sovereign."[50]

Mill cautioned against social interference because he held that society could exercise tyranny more formidable than despotism.

Expansionist nationalism was rejected by the sane masses in the West long ago, but still, some of the Western governments were going ahead with their secret wars undermining democracy in poorer countries, particularly in the developing countries in Asia, Africa and far-off Latin America between the two world wars or even at the present moment. In our own country, Naxalism has not yet become totally irrelevant. Naxalism, however, is not the only extra-parliamentary opposition to the Indian polity. If one looks back to the distant past, on

---

50 On Liberty: John Stuart Mill (1806-1873) J S Mill was trained by his father James Mill as well as by John Austin. In his early days, he was influenced by Bentham's utilitarianism philosophy and its reforming programmes. He was of the opinion that happiness of man cannot be sought as an end in itself; cultivation of feeling is necessary for proper development of man.

7 November 1966, an army of *Gaurakshaks* (cow protectors) had stormed the Parliament.

Former Prime Minister Nehru had warned his secretaries of Government of India in his last meeting with them, as Y D Gundevia recalls in his memoirs, *Outside the Archives*, "The danger to India, mark you is not communism. It is Hindu right-wing communalism." Even in the wake of the Babri Masjid demolition, L K Advaniji later admitted the movement was not religious but political.[51]

Gandhiji never accepted India's division on religious lines. His whole life was dedicated to Hindu-Muslim unity. Gandhiji is not just the Father of our Nation, he was also the maker of our nation. Communal unity and harmony is the bedrock of India's strength and the key to its glorious future. Gandhiji believed in the intrinsic power of Hinduism, of assimilation, evaluation and adaptation as it was inclusive and offered space for the presence of people from every faith. He declared that no faith could be in danger in India because India had always been the homeland for every faith.

M J Akbar's new book *Gandhi's Hinduism, The Struggle against Jinnah's Islam* strongly emphasises the fact that Gandhiji fought for the unity of India for every moment of his public life. This book clearly analyses the history of Partition and demonstrates the inherent spiritual secularism that Gandhiji stood for and the divisive colour that Jinnah gave to religion only to secure political ends. This is the sum-total view of the former President of India Pranab Mukherjee as expressed in releasing the new book recently.[52]

---

51 Fifty years of the Rise of the Right Apoorvanand, Teacher University of Delhi. Outlook. 6 November,2017. Fifty years of the Rise of the Right, Apoorvanand, Teacher, University of Delhi. Outlook. 6 November, 2017.

52 Op.cit. Assam Tribune, February 10,2020

The model of a single language, a shared religion and a common enemy is the model by which nations were created throughout Europe. Ali Jinnah insisted that the Muslims could not live with Hindus, so they needed their own homeland. Hatred of India has been an intrinsic factor to the very idea of Pakistan since its inception. However, if we view Indian culture there is no place for chauvinism. In India, there has been catholicity of mind and spirit though there might be aberration now and then, which is few and far between. B R Ambedkar in his Constituent Assembly speech said, "In India, 'Bhakti' (Devotion) plays a part in its politics unequalled in magnitude by the part it plays in politics of any other country in the world. Bhakti in religion may be a road to the salvation of the soul. But in politics, Bhakti or hero-worship is a sure road to degradation and to eventual dictatorship." One should remember that no leader in any country is perfect and infallible.

As for India, ours is a mosaic of nationalism that is the fusion of a plurality of cultures, religions, traditions, customs and social mores, like a garden where different varieties of flowers bloom, depicting the splendid unity and harmony.

In the Hind Swaraj, Gandhiji drew on the ancient idea of *Bharatvarsha* or India's nationalism. He said our ancestors who established Rameshwaram Setubandhan in the South, Jagannath Temple in the East and Haridwar in the North were no fools. He asserted that the ancestors knew that the worship of God could have been performed at home as well and yet they argued that there must be one nation and established holy places in various parts of the country imbued with an idea of composite nationality. Even the advent of Muslims could not make any difference because they would be assimilated into the mainstream. Aurobindo was also of the view that a nation is not just a creed or religion. It is, after all, a way of life.

Machiavelli was the first of modern totalitarian thinkers who believed in the potency of material interests rather than spiritual ones and may be said to have inspired Karl Marx in his materialistic interpretation of history. He is the first exponent with his theory of aggrandisement, which is the basis of the modern theory of power politics on which much has been written by thinkers like Nietzsche, Treitschke and others. Whereas Hegel views the state as the march of God on earth, which is not far away from the conception of Machiavelli. Machiavelli not only separated morality from politics but also relegated religion to a very subordinate position in his political system and it is because of this we think that modern study of politics begins with him.

For centuries, politics and religion have been intertwined. Politics, in fact, was the handmaid of religion. Some of the best medieval thinkers subordinated the state to the church. As a political realist, Machiavelli realised passive Christian virtues. He, however, knew the public utility of the binding force of religion without which the state could not exist and be looked upon. Devotion to religion was a useful weapon in the hands of a statesman, to be skilfully used in furtherance of the end of the state, but not above it or beside it. He must be reckoned as the last of the great line of medieval secularists who urged the subordination of the church to the state. Machiavelli stood on the borderline between the middle and modern ages. He ushered in the modern age by ridding politics of the tutelage of religion.

Long ago, Einstein said, "Nationalism is an infantile disease. It is the measles of mankind." Infatuation with wild patriotism is nothing short of craze for a country or its people. It boils down to madness, a sort of fantasy or illusion. Patriotism is said to be the very basis of nationalism. But then how can you know that a man is really a patriot but in his heart of hearts, he may not be. It is something spiritual, which cannot be implanted on a man or woman. It may sometimes be hybrid nationalism that divides people rather than uniting them. It is, therefore, a bellicose nationalism that is not capable of fulfilling the aspirations of people.

Very recently, a shooter with far-right beliefs killed nine people at a bar and café in Germany, not far away from Frankfurt. All the victims were of Kurdish origin. This is nothing but sheer xenophobic nationalism that led the German Chancellor, Angela Merkel, to remark, "Racism is a poison, hatred is a poison and this poison exists in society and it is already responsible for too many crimes."[53]

Rise of jingoism or bellicose nationalism is a global phenomenon manifest in the rise of such leaders like Donald Trump, the President of the USA, Recep Tayyip Erdogan of Turkey or Mahathir Mohammad of Malaysia and the like who pursue a xenophobic, paranoid, often hateful form of nationalism. Another factor for the rise of extreme nationalism is the rise of Islamic fundamentalism in our backyard as well as in the Arab world. This view is shared by no lesser a person than the noted historian and thinker Rama Chandra Guha, which is manifest in his well-written article, *Patriotism vs Jingoism* in *The Outlook.*[54]

In this context, I think that the Indian Constitution needs to be so amended that India becomes an indestructible nation of indestructible states like the USA. Otherwise, with the rise of bellicose nationalism, India is very prone to further Balkanisation like the tiny states of present-day Europe.

Hence, it is true to say as in the words of Spengler, "Nations are neither linguistic nor political nor biological but spiritual unities."[55]

I conclude this piece with the words of the celebrated poet of France of the bygone years France Preseren (1800–1849):

"God's blessings on all nations,

---

53   Op.cit. Angela Merkel, Chancellor of Germany. Assam Tribune.21 February, 2020.

54   Op.cit Rama Chandra Guha. Outlook. February,5, 2018.

55   R M MacIver: The Modern State.

Who long and work for that bright day,

Whenever earth habitations

No war, no strife shall its

Sway;

Who long to see

That all men free

No more shall foes, but

Neighbours be."

EPILOGUE

In today's world, no nation can survive in isolation. A nation, however big and powerful, must be inclusive domestically and in relation to other nations on a cooperative spirit. In the international sphere, a nation needs to be guided by the ideal principle of mutual co-existence, so beautifully and eminently enunciated by the late former Prime Minister of India, Jawaharlal Nehru at the Afro-Asian Conference in Bandung (Indonesia) as early as 1955. These principles came to be better known as the *Panchsheel*, or the five principles of mutual co-existence, which formed the very basis of deliberation at the conference.[56]

No doubt, as a concept, non-alignment is a sound concept in international affairs. However, the fact of the matter is that during war or emergency, no nation can afford to remain non-aligned or

---

56   This refers to the Bandung Afro-Asian Conference in Indonesia held in 1955. This conference chalked out five principles of co-existence enunciated by the then Prime Minister of India. These principles are also known as the Panchsheel. In this conference, resolutions were passed opposing any form of colonization in the world. The main features of these principles are hereunder:

   i)   Respect for the territorial sovereignty and political independence of all nations

   ii)   Non-aggression

   iii)   Non-interference in the domestic affairs of other nations

   iv)   Settlement of all disputes through peaceful means through negotiations

   v)   Mutual co-existence

neutral under the prevailing world circumstances. It will, therefore, be obliged to take a stand dictated by abnormal situations. However, during normal times, a nation may opt for non-alignment and avoid entanglement with any other power or powers. As a lofty principle, a nation may follow a policy of disarmament, though no nation affords to take risks when all others are well armed.

Moreover, though we are said to be living in an Atomic Age, we can avoid the production of nuclear weapons like ICBM, which pose the gravest danger to world peace and security. We can easily restrain the manufacturing of these deadly weapons for the sake of peace and security and for the much greater cause of humanity at large. We have ourselves been the holocaust caused by the nuclear bombs, killing millions of innocent people of Hiroshima and Nagasaki in the wake of World War II in 1945. As a matter of fact and principle, nations should willingly desist from producing such nuclear warheads, which may cause untold sufferings and massive devastations unleashed by the nations at war. What is much more, this danger is compounded by the fact that when these weapons of mass destruction fall into the hands of terrorists, the situation will be aggravated beyond measure and go out of control. This will definitely be suicidal for the succeeding generations of humankind, which the Almighty God forbid.

There is yet another significant arena in which nations of the world should unite. As the wise saying goes 'United we stand, divided we fall.' This applies to not only trade and commerce among civilised nations but also to the emerging problem of global warming and climate change, which is now one of the main concerns of the people and the future of the planet. We all want a liveable planet to live in. But things are passing in such a manner that a day will not be far off when the people of this planet will not be able to live a healthy life anymore. As to trade and commerce, the same principle of give and take and moderation must be in place among nations. There must be proper access to the markets. There should not be lengthy and clumsy procedures in the import or export spheres. All should be hassle-free. Nations must rid themselves of unnecessary agricultural or non-agricultural trade barriers. Intellectual property rights, patents, trademarks, quality of commodities or products should be adhered to, so that there may not be any unholy trade practices. A proper environment should be created so that trade and business flourish among nations unhindered and in a harmonious manner. Today, there is a prevalence of what we call bio-piracy in most of the Latin American countries. It should be banned.

There is, at present, a category of legal provisions in the existing WTO agreement that gives developing countries greater flexibility with regard to the application of commitments and the use of policy instruments and developed countries the right to treat the developing countries more favourably. Moreover, special safeguard mechanisms for developing countries raised in the Doha round of negotiations recognises that developing nations have the right to temporarily increase tariffs in the face of import surges.

Former US Secretary of State Henry Kissinger warned that an armed conflict could break out between the USA and China if they fail to resolve their trade war. The sober remarks from Kissinger, who was instrumental in normalising diplomatic relations between Washington and Beijing, came at a conference in Beijing on the future of economic giants. "If conflict is permitted to run unconstrained, the outcome could be even worse than it was in Europe," he said in the Bloomberg New Economy Forum.[57]

World War I broke out because of a relatively minor crisis. And today the weapons are more powerful. China and the USA have been caught in a trade dispute for the last eighteen or more months, with the two

---

57 Assam Tribune News, November, 2019.

sides struggling to reach an agreement despite a series of negotiations. Tensions have been running high on the diplomatic front.

Beijing has lashed out at Washington over USA naval operations in the disputed South China Sea. USA's criticism of China's mass detention of ethnic Uighurs and US Congress' support for pro-democracy protestors in Hong Kong was vehemently protested by China. "China is a major economic power and so are we," Kissinger is known to have said. "And we are bound to step into each other's toes all over the world."

During the Cold War between the USA and the Soviet Union, a plan to reduce the nuclear capability of both the countries was on top priority. But in China, unlike the former conflict between the two, which had been passive, there is no framework to deal with Beijing as a military power. "If the two sides keep seeing every issue in the world on the terms of conflict with each other, it could be dangerous for mankind," Kissinger added.[58]

Kissinger said that trade negotiations were just a substitute for more substantial talks about conflicts between the two, including tensions over Hong Kong. When asked if the unrest in the semi-autonomous region of China could be the flashpoint for a new Cold War, Kissinger said he hoped the highly emotional issue would be settled by the negotiations.[59]

It may be recalled that former President Nixon's Secretary of State flew secretly to Beijing in 1971 to begin talks on new relations between the USA and China.

USA President Donald Trump did not veto the Hong Kong Human Rights and Democracy Act 2019 as anticipated, which was recently

---

58   Ibid, Assam Tribune News, 24 November, 2019.

59   Ibid

passed by both the Chambers of US Congress with almost unanimous support.

The new legislation would force President Trump to assess whether political unrest in the vital financial hub justifies changing its unique treatment under the USA law. The Act would require the Secretary of State, at least once in a year, to see to it that Hong Kong still retains enough autonomy to warrant the special USA trading consideration that bolsters its status as world financial hub.

The USA treats the semi-autonomous Hong Kong, which has its own legal and political systems, differently from the Chinese mainland, when it comes to trade and export controls.

Acting USA Assistant Secretary of State for South and Central Asia, Alice Well, said at the Wilson Centre Think Tank recently that there are reasons to question Chinese largesse through the One Belt One Road initiative. The American diplomat has said and alleged that Beijing has never supported the globally recognised transparent lending practices.[60]

Across the world and in South and Central Asia, China is pressing countries to sign One Belt One Road deals, emphasising peace, openness, inclusive mutual lending and cooperation. That sounds well. But after seeing One Belt One Road practices for the last few years, there are reasons to question the Chinese largesse. For example, China offers substantial financing usually as loans, but Beijing is not a member of the Paris Club and has never supported globally recognised transparent lending practices. According to an estimate released by the ICSID (International Centre for Settlement of Investment Disputes), China is the world's largest official creditor, lending over five trillion USA dollars worldwide, but it does not publish or even report overall figures on its official lending records. So rating agencies like the Paris Club or the IMF are not able to monitor these financial transactions.

---

60   Ibid (Assam Tribune News, 24 November, 2019)

Chinese communist party officials now recognise that they need to use the language of openness and accountability, but the fact remains that the country stands outside global efforts, including those of the IMF and the World Bank to improve transparency that enhances policy-making, prevents fiscal crises and deters corruption.

It is relevant here to recapitulate the speech delivered by former Prime Minister of India, Jawaharlal Nehru at the plenary session of the Asian Relations Conference in New Delhi in March 1947. This speech is still very relevant for the people of Asia and beyond. He said, "May I say here that this conference and the idea underlying this is no way aggressive or against any other continent or country. However, ever since the news of this conference went abroad, some people in Europe and America have viewed it with doubt, imagining that this was some kind of a Pan Asian Movement against somebody. Ours is the great design of promoting peace and progress all over the world."[61]

The countries of Asia can no longer be used as pawns by others; they are bound to have their own policies in world affairs. In this Atomic and Cyber Age, Asia will have to function effectively in the maintenance of peace. Indeed, there can be no peace unless Asia plays its part. There is today conflict in many countries, and all of us in Asia are full of our own problems.

Nevertheless, the whole spirit and outlook of Asia are peaceful and the emergence of Asia in world affairs will be a powerful influence for world peace. We have arrived at a stage in human affairs when the ideal of One World or some kind of a World Federation seems to be essential, though this idea may be far-fetched or utopian because there are obstacles in the way for its realisation. Anyway, for the moment, we must support the UNO as a unifying force for achieving our desired goals.

61　Selected works of Nehru, the Ex PM of India, Second Series, 1984.

www.ingramcontent.com/pod-product-compliance
Lightning Source LLC
Chambersburg PA
CBHW051212250726
48655CB00006B/2373